STORIES FROM THE MINES

STORIES FROM THE MINES

IN THE HEART OF THE MINER WAS THE SOUL-ROOTED
DETERMINATION TO STARVE TO THE LAST CRUST OF BREAD
AND FIGHT OUT THE LONG, DREARY BATTLE TO THE END,
IN ORDER TO WIN A LIFE FOR A CHILD AND SECURE FOR IT
A PLACE IN THE WORLD IN KEEPING WITH ADVANCING
CIVILIZATION. —John Mitchell, president of the anthracite miner's union

Library of Congress Cataloging-in-Publication Data

Curra, Thomas M., 1960-
    Stories from the mines / Thomas M. Curra, Greg Matkosky.
        p. cm.
    ISBN 1-58966-051-X (hc) — ISBN 1-58966-050-1 (pbk.)
    1. Anthracite coal industry—Pennsylvania—History. 2. Coal mines and
mining—Pennsylvania—History. 3. Coal miners—Pennsylvania—History. I. Matkosky,
Greg, 1958-II. Title.

HD9547.P4 C77 2002
338.2'725'09748—dc21   20022073259

PRINTED IN CANADA

Photo Credits

Table of Contents
Miners standing in the cage; courtesy of the Lackawanna Historical Society

Foreword
Miners with a goat; courtesy of the Luzerne County Historical Society, Children;
courtesy of the Luzerne County Historical Society, Multi-language warning sign;
courtesy of the Luzerne County Historical Society, Family group photo; courtesy
of the Luzerne County Historical Society

Chapter One
Coal delivery wagon; courtesy of the Lackawanna Historical Society, Drawing of
anthracite coal canal activity at Port Carbon; courtesy of the Hagley Museum, The
barge known as "Bird" in an anthracite canal; courtesy of the Historical Society
of Schuylkill County, Miners loading a mine car; courtesy of the Lackawanna
Historical Society, Portrait of J.P. Morgan; courtesy of the Library of Congress,
Turbine room in a Long Island power plant; courtesy of the Hagley Museum,
Coal stove; courtesy of the Luzerne County Historical Society, Newspaper image
"All Mines Idle"; courtesy of Times Shamrock, Family portrait; courtesy of Ann
Andrichak Matkosky, Group and tree swing; courtesy of the Luzerne County
Historical Society, Baseball team photo; courtesy of the Luzerne County Historical
Society, Ellis Island processing room; courtesy of the Library of Congress, People
boarding a train; courtesy of the Luzerne County Historical Society

Chapter Two
Women with children sitting in wheel barrows; courtesy of the Historical Society
of Schuylkill County, Mother and children; courtesy of the Historical Society of
Schuylkill County, Portrait of William Jennings Bryan; courtesy of the Library
of Congress, Northeastern Pennsylvania landscape; courtesy of the Luzerne County
Historical Society, Miners sitting on a coal train; courtesy of the Lackawanna

Historical Society, Mother Jones at mine entrance; courtesy of the Historical
Society of Schuylkill County, Newspaper image "Troops Called Out"; courtesy
of Times Shamrock, Boy standing on a dirt road leading into a company town;
courtesy of the Lackawanna Historical Society, A barber serves a group of men
outside; courtesy of the Historical Society of Schuylkill County

Chapter Three
Breaker boys and cracker boss, also called a chute boss ; courtesy of the Hagley
Museum, Cracker boss and breaker boys; courtesy of the Lackawanna Historical
Society, Portrait of John Mitchell; courtesy of the Historical Society of Schuylkill
County, Dickson Colliery; courtesy of the Lackawanna Historical Society, Breaker;
courtesy of the Luzerne County Historical Society, Westmoreland anthracite coal
breaker; courtesy of the Library of Congress, Miner in casket surrounded by
family; courtesy of the Historical Society of Schuylkill County, Injured miner
calling for help; courtesy of the Luzerne County Historical Society, Miner drilling
into a coal seam; courtesy of the Lackawanna Historical Society, South Side
Scranton Westmoreland coal mine 1899; courtesy of the Hagley Museum, Newspaper image "Strike Is Declared Off"; courtesy of Times Shamrock, Boys waiting
for the paymaster; courtesy of the Lackawanna Historical Society, "backyard" of
a company house; courtesy of the Luzerne County Historical Society, company
currency, also called "scrip"; courtesy of the Historical Society of Schuylkill
County, butcher shop; courtesy of the Luzerne County Historical Society, family
standing in front of a coal town church; courtesy of the Luzerne County Historical
Society, John Mitchell seated with Bishop Hoban and President Roosevelt; courtesy
of Times Shamrock, Father Curran with President Roosevelt; courtesy of the
Luzerne County Historical Society

Chapter Four
Portrait of Philadelphia Coal and Iron Company president George Baer; courtesy
of the Hagley Museum, Telegram to John Mitchell from George Baer; courtesy
of the Hagley Museum, Exterior shot of the Delaware, Lackawanna and Western
railroad yard; courtesy of the Library of Congress, Man with a rifle guarding coal
cars; courtesy of the Luzerne County Historical Society, Man leaning against the

breaker with the tipple above him; courtesy of the Hagley Museum, Newspaper
image "Mitchell On The Stand"; courtesy of Times Shamrock, Illustration of the
first trip of the Stourbridge Lion steam locomotive; courtesy of the Library of
Congress, Two miners standing aboveground; courtesy of the Luzerne County
Historical Society, Three miners standing underground; courtesy of the Luzerne
County Historical Society

Chapter Five
The Lackawanna County Courthouse in Scranton, Pennsylvania 1902; courtesy of
the Library of Congress, Portrait of President Theodore Roosevelt; courtesy of the
Library of Congress, Anthracite Coal Mine Commission in courtroom #3 of the
Lackawanna County Courthouse; courtesy of the Historical Society of Schuylkill
County, Large group of soldiers in formation in city street; courtesy of the Luzerne
County Historical Society, Children behind company housing; courtesy of the
Luzerne County Historical Society, Newspaper advertisement for the John Mitchell
brand condensed milk; courtesy of Times Shamrock, Mule pulling a mine car;
courtesy of the Lackawanna Historical Society, Group of miners posing outside a
mine entrance; courtesy of the Luzerne County Historical Society

Chapter Six
The Anthracite Coal Strike Commissioners arriving in Scranton; courtesy of the
Library of Congress, Boy with shovel and dog; courtesy of the Hagley Museum Coal
train; courtesy of the Luzerne County Historical Society, Miner standing at gate;
courtesy of the Hagley Museum, Newspaper image "Award Of The Commission"; courtesy of Times Shamrock, People picnicking across the river from a breaker; courtesy
of the Luzerne County Historical Society, Boy miners; courtesy of the Luzerne
County Historical Society, Children sleighriding; courtesy of the Luzerne County
Historical Society, Crowd for John Mitchell's funeral outside the cathedral in
Scranton; courtesy of Times Shamrock, Scranton family estate mansion; courtesy
of the University of Scranton

CONTENTS

FOREWORD BY JOHN W. COSGROVE

EXECUTIVE DIRECTOR LACKAWANNA HERITAGE VALLEY AUTHORITY

The Lackawanna Heritage Valley Authority works in partnership with individuals as well as civic, business and government organizations to improve the economic vitality of communities along the Lackawanna River in northeastern Pennsylvania and preserve for future generations the important story of how the anthracite coal industry shaped the Lackawanna Valley and the United States.

More than 100 years ago, the eyes of the nation and the eyes of the world were fixed intently on the remarkable people of northeastern Pennsylvania's anthracite region. It was so because it fell to them to perform the backbreaking work of fueling the extraordinary industrial growth of the United States of America. They rose to the task with uncommon fortitude, unbounded energy, and an unbridled spirit.

These people, emigrating from twenty countries, came to northeastern Pennsylvania to escape poverty and persecution, to build a future filled with hope and opportunity. They ended up building a new nation, the strongest and wealthiest nation that the world has ever known. All they really asked for in return was to be treated fairly,

Grade school children in Wilkes-Barre. An important legacy of the anthracite coal region is the protection of children from labor exploitation. Federal child labor laws inspired by the abuse of children who worked in the anthracite mines helped advance the idea that the most effective child labor legislation was actually compulsory education for forty weeks a year.

with dignity, in a place where their dreams could be achieved, and where they and their children could live free.

Stories From The Mines endeavors to again fix the focus on the extraordinary people of the anthracite region and the lasting positive impact that their grueling labors had on our world. This valuable book has been produced from the collective efforts of many, many creative and generous minds. It tells the stories of those who came before us— our mothers and our fathers, our grandmothers and our grandfathers, and beyond. These are stories that the ancestors of all immigrants to America can take great pride.

Their story is our story.

We are the children for whom they sought a better life.

It is our duty to honor them. It is our responsibility to learn these stories and to retell them today with fairness and dignity and genuine pride. Let us learn from this glorious past, revel in the lives we lead today because of it, and lean on our proud heritage to propel us to a vibrant future.

NOTICE

IF YOU ARE INJURED, NO MATTER HOW LITTLE, TE[L]
YOUR FOREMAN ABOUT IT RIGHT AWAY.

ZUR KENNTNISNAHME

BENACHRICHTIGEN SIE IHREN WERKFUHRER SOFORT
WENN IHNEN AUCH NUR DER GERINGFUGISTE UNFALL
[Z]UGESTOSSEN IST.

FIGYELMEZTETÉS

HA MEGSÉRULT, LEGYEN AZ BÁRMILYEN CSEKÉLY IS
AZONNAL JELENTSE BE AZ ELÓMUNKÁSÁNÁL.

AVVERTENZA

SE VI SIETE FATTO MALE, ANCHE SE LEGGERMENTE
DITELO SUBITO AL VOSTRO FOREMAN.

OBJAVA

AKO SI MA I NAJMANJE OZLIJEDJEN KAŽI TO ODMAH
[S]VOMU NADSTOJNIKU (FORMANU).

POZOR

AKO SE POŠKODUJETE, ČE TUDI LE MALO, POVEJTE
TAKOJ SVOJEMU FORMANU.

BACZNOŚĆ

JEZELI ZOSTANIESZ POKALECZONYM, NIE ROBI[L]
[R]ÓZNICY JAK TRYWIALNIE, DAJ ZNAC NATYCHMIAS[T]
[SW]EM FORMANOWI.

(left) This safety sign posted in an anthracite mine warning miners in seven languages to report any injury is a reflection of the anthracite region's intense ethnic diversity at the beginning of the 20th century. (right) In 1900, the poverty line was calculated to be about $460.00 a year for a family of five in the industrial communities of New England and the Mid-Atlantic states. At this same time, the average miner's salary was between $400.00 and $600.00. Many employees earned less than this, while supporting a family of more than five members. About 5% of all mine employees made above $800.00 a year.

1762
Connecticut pioneers discover anthracite coal in the Wyoming Valley.

1769
Obadiah Gore uses anthracite in a smithing forge.

1775
Regular use of anthracite as a fuel occurs in Pittston.

1776
The Declaration of Independence is signed in Philadelphia.

1778
Judge Jesse Fell makes the first metallurgical use of anthracite for nails in Wilkes-Barre.

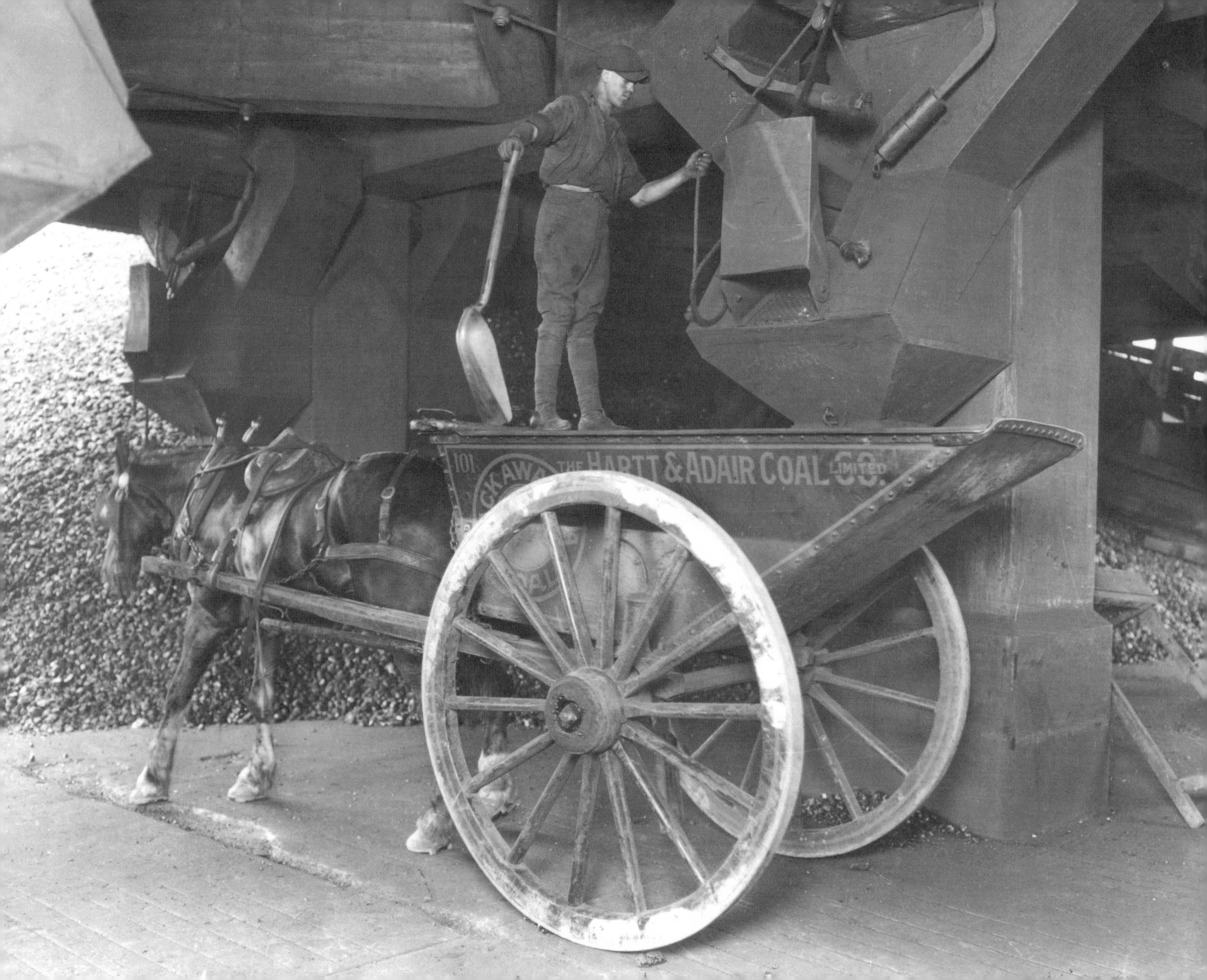
101
THE HARTT & ADAIR COAL CO.
LIMITED

A FEW MEN IN THIS COUNTRY ARE CHARGED WITH THE
TERRIBLE OFFENSE OF BEING VERY RICH. I OWE THE PUBLIC NOTHING.
—J.P. Morgan, financier and industrial organizer

CHAPTER 1

A hundred years ago, America inaugurated the 20th century with a raucous epoch of unrestrained capitalism based on the politics of business. A surge of great industrial monopolies deconstructed the Declaration of Independence into the broken promise of a young democracy. Consequently, working men, women and children became exploited, and the opportunity promised by the Statue of Liberty was denied to many, for the advantage of the few.

Nowhere was this more evident than in lives of the people who worked in the anthracite coal mines of northeastern Pennsylvania, a place where immigration and industrialization drove America's industrial revolution and ignited the country's ascendancy as the most powerful nation the world has ever known. The story of these immigrant anthracite miners and their families inspired a

Coal delivery wagons like the one in this picture were a common sight in cities and towns throughout the eastern seaboard. By the end of the 19th century, anthracite coal was used as a domestic and industrial fuel at the rate of one ton per year for each of the region's 35 million inhabitants.

conflict of social forces that dug into the source of power stretching from Wall Street to Pennsylvania Avenue, and stirred the American people to serve justice in a place where sunlight has never reached. Against the backdrop of America's evolution as the world's dominant superpower in the 20th century, the conflicting interests of capitalism collided with the discourse of people dedicated to restoring human rights sacrificed in the country's effort to secure its position in the world. In this historic struggle, the weapon both wielded was—anthracite coal.

Between 1810 and 1910, anthracite became a necessity of commerce, and a strategic resource spawning an industrial empire that helped America become less reliant on Europe for key industrial goods like iron and steel. Along with a windfall of foreign investment and immigrant labor from around the world, the United States evolved from an agrarian to an industrial society.

America's growing prosperity at the end of the 19th century was an economic consequence of the increased use of anthracite early in the country's industrial revolution. Because anthracite is almost pure carbon, it burned hotter than any other existing fuel. When used in early blast furnaces to smelt iron ore, this property helped to create stronger grades of steel that liberated American industry in the 1830s and 1840s. At that time, anthracite coal cost less and survived shipping better than charcoal, wasn't affected by weather, and produced a more efficient heat. It was also easy to use. As American cities began to run out of

wood and charcoal as a heating and cooking fuel, anthracite coal became an essential alternative.

Throughout the 19th century, anthracite was used to fuel power systems in factories, which led to the large labor forces and the non-stop integrated process of the modern factory system. This stimulated unprecedented investments in construction and transportation, produced a degree of specialization and standardization that fused a growing consumer demand to the country's industrial revolution, and sustained America's high rate of upward mobility at the end of the 19th century. By that time, anthracite was fueling power in steam plants for transportation systems, gas production, and electric lighting.

Anthracite coal played an influential role in establishing fuel-intensive industries like food processing, textiles, papermaking and chemicals, which were established within areas serviced by railroads that transported anthracite. The machine tool industry was born to support the industrialization spurred by advancements in production. Successful anthracite canal, rail and mining enterprises provided a model for corporations in the early industrial era. By the start of the 20th century, the United States overtook Great Britain

Virtually all of the estimated one billion tons of anthracite coal mined from beneath northeastern Pennsylvania by 1900 was extracted by hand.

as "Workshop of the World". Anthracite was also accessible. Though it existed in Great Britain and Europe, as well as in New England, the Southeast and Southwest, virtually all known reserves in the world existed under only five geologically diverse counties and 1400 square miles of northeastern Pennsylvania.

With half of the country's population living within 300 miles of these centralized deposits at the end of the 19th century, industrialists in New York City created giant integrated firms to launch America's industrial revolution in coal and iron, and dominate the world's largest upwardly mobile mass market.

These combinations, or monopolies, were great interstate corporations created and centrally administered by stock-promoting directors instead of individual entrepreneurs. Between 1789 and 1889, American industry produced 12 combinations with a total value of one billion dollars. In the following 11 years, 236 trusts were created with a capital of more than six billion dollars, the most massive and rapid burst of wealth the world had ever seen.

Industrialists rallied around the idea of Social Darwinism, which compared business to nature. That is, the strongest survive, and the weakest do not. John Rockefeller, America's first billionaire, said, "Combination is not an evil tendency in business. It is merely the working out of a law of

John Pierpont Morgan played an important role in the creation of such American corporations as General Electric, United States Steel and numerous railroads. In 1895, his bank loaned the federal government more than sixty million dollars to stem a worsening national economic depression.

nature and a law of God." Even inventor Thomas Edison remarked, "I measure everything by the size of a silver dollar. If it don't come up to that standard then I know it's no good."

Another industrialist who agreed with Edison's standard was John Pierpont Morgan, the world's most powerful banker, and some believed even more powerful than the President of the United States. J.P. Morgan had three rules for conducting business: his company must dominate the board of directors, competition must be subdued, and costs must be minimized. Following Thomas Edison's advice, Morgan would sell the Edison General Electric Company out from under the inventor himself, and remove his name from the corporation's title.

J.P. Morgan loved the bible and art. He collected priceless European art treasures and artifacts with the same meticulousness that he collected corporations, and used them to help establish New York City's Metropolitan Museum of Art and American Museum of Natural History. Though he inherited wealth, Morgan created his own fortune from holding 72 directorships in 47 corporations. By 1900, one sixth of the country's railroad tracks would be under his control or influence, at a time when more than half of all the issues on the New York Stock Exchange were railroads.

Morgan created a "community of interest" in the anthracite coal fields that ultimately consisted of six different railroad companies: the Philadelphia and Reading, the Central of New Jersey, the Erie, the Lehigh Valley, the Delaware and Hudson, and the Pennsylvania. This combination created a national demand for anthracite, controlled prices, wages and working conditions from corporate offices in Philadelphia and Manhattan, and produced profits from both mining and shipping.

Morgan enjoyed playing solitaire. Lonely and lordly, he once said: "A few men in this country are charged with the terrible offense of being very rich. I owe the public nothing." From his grand

1780–1800
Efforts fail to entice Philadelphia inhabitants to use anthracite over firewood.

1789
George Washington wins first presidential election. Four million citizen vote, mostly concentrated on the eastern seaboard.

1792
Lehigh Coal Mine Company is formed.

1804
Anthracite discovered in Carbondale by Samuel Preston.

1807
Abijah Smith establishes the first coal company in Wyoming Valley, Plymouth.

AND WHILE THE LAW [OF COMPETITION] MAY BE SOMETIMES HARD FOR THE INDIVIDUAL, IT IS BEST FOR THE RACE, BECAUSE IT ENSURES THE SURVIVAL OF THE FITTEST IN EVERY DEPARTMENT.

—Andrew Carnegie

mahogany-paneled library at 219 Madison Avenue in New York City, he clearly understood what National Geographic magazine wrote about the anthracite country of northeastern Pennsylvania: "One who has not wandered through the seemingly endless reaches of the innumerable man-made caverns of the coal regions, and there studied first hand the tremendous industry of harvesting the solidified sunbeams planted for humanity by a bounteous Providence in the Carboniferous Age, cannot appreciate the vastness of that industry nor its meaning to the American people."

That meaning, though, would prove to be written on sand. And from across the Atlantic, a wind of change was about to rise, and carry upon it a new face for the young nation that would transform the meaning of anthracite coal, and profoundly affect the course of American history.

(right) Despite the hardships and miseries encountered in the anthracite communities, many immigrants built a life in northeastern Pennsylvania, and this drew even more family members from the old country to the region. (far right) Because anthracite coal produced an efficient heat that did not create air pollution problems, it was the popular fuel for industrial and domestic applications in the heavily industrialized and populated northeast and Midwest.

SHORT STORIES FROM THE MINES

Location, Location, Location

Coal's Golden Age occurred between 1860 and 1920. Two distinct coalfields developed in the United States—the bituminous fields of eastern Virginia, western Pennsylvania, and western Maryland, and the anthracite fields of northeastern Pennsylvania.

By this time, the East Coast consumed more than one-third of U.S. anthracite production, over 35 million tons. Most of this was used for domestic heating, as anthracite coal gave off very little smoke when burned compared to bituminous coal. Pennsylvania, New York and New Jersey accounted for 65% of the East Coast market. New York City was burning 9 million tons, Philadelphia over 4 million tons, and Boston 2 million tons.

The Original Black Gold

The earliest use of coal in America occurred in a blacksmith forge in Richmond, Virginia, in 1702. Fifty years later, bituminous mines there became the first working mines in the colonies. By the middle 1700's, settlers from Connecticut adventured south, and found anthracite coal in exposed outcrops in northeastern Pennsylvania. During the Revolutionary War, blacksmiths in the region discovered this "hard coal" produced a heat that could create stronger iron products. No one knew it then, but America was taking its first steps as an industrial superpower.

When eastern forests became unable to supply enough firewood for nearby Philadelphia and New York, companies formed to dig canals that linked the anthracite mines to rivers that flowed to these cities. By the mid-1800's, the anthracite canal system became America's first high capacity, low cost inland transportation system, and created a speculative fever comparable to the California gold rush.

The Politics of Coal

During the anthracite era, which lasted from approximately 1835 to 1940, the United States was transformed from fundamentally an agricultural nation dependent upon wood as its primary material into an industrialized nation dependent upon iron. Anthracite coal played a crucial role in America's early industrialization by providing a fuel for the country's burgeoning iron industry. Without iron, railroads could not have been built. Railroad growth in the latter part of the 19th century could be considered almost the equivalent to the dot-com explosion of late 20th century. Without the railroads, the United States would not have had a national transportation network to join the resources of the Midwest and Northeast and create the political unity that enabled the United States to survive the Civil War as one nation. Anthracite coal was also the primary heating and cooking fuel in the northeastern United States.

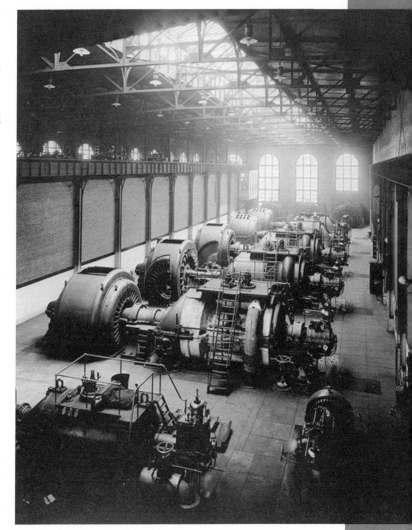

BETTER, FASTER, CHEAPER

Between 1814 and 1842, anthracite would be shipped over roads to canal heads in towns like Honesdale, Port Carbon and Pottsville. Where longer distances separated the mines from the canals, gravity powered railroads transported coal to the canals. Mules would ride down the mountain with the anthracite, sometimes over distances of 10 miles and elevation changes of 500 feet, and then pull the empty coal cars back up to the mine.

At the canal heads, boats loaded with sixty tons of anthracite were also pulled by mules or horses, and young boys walked alongside the animals to guide them for the 25 miles a boat could cover in a day. The canals connected anthracite mines with the Susquehanna, Lehigh and Delaware rivers. A trip from Pottsville to New York took 7 days. The Schuylkill Canal became the busiest waterway in the U.S., and made anthracite coal northeastern

Pennsylvania's dominant export, transforming the region's economic and social base from farming to mining. The canals, however, would not fare the transition as well.

When railroad engineers solved construction and operational problems and designed mechanical systems so it became cheaper to ship anthracite by train, the canals slowly went out of business, like many other entrepreneurial firms to come who would attempt to compete with a mounting coal and rail combination.

(below) A drawing of a canal head from the early 19th century, where coal trains brought the anthracite from the mines to boats that would take the coal to markets such as Philadelphia and New York. By the 1860's, railroads were constructed to ship anthracite coal to these markets faster, cheaper and more reliably. (left) An immigrant family from the anthracite region of Pennsylvania.

1812

The War of 1812 cuts off Virginia coal. Firewood prices rise, spurring the use of anthracite as a cooking and heating fuel.

1815

The Lackawanna region begins to supply the Philadelphia market with anthracite.

1815

The first use of anthracite in the U.S. to manufacture iron occurs in Pottsville.

1820

The Lehigh Coal and Navigation Company is formed. The U.S. Geological Survey identifies this as the official beginning of the anthracite industry, and also of the industrial revolution in America. Anthracite mined in the first year: 36 tons.

1822

Anthracite mining begins in the Schuylkill region.

THE LABOR MOVEMENT IS A COMMAND FROM GOD ALMIGHTY HIMSELF!
—Mother Jones, labor activist

CHAPTER 2

No other place in the world has ever possessed such a monopoly on a natural resource as northeastern Pennsylvania does with anthracite coal. By the beginning of the 20th century, the region had evolved into four trade zones, distinguished by the geographic dimensions of four immense anthracite deposits and by the market where the coal was sold. These coal deposits existed principally within five counties: Carbon, Lackawanna, Luzerne, Northumberland and Schuylkill. The Schuylkill district alone had over 2000 miles of tunnels.

The city of Scranton was nicknamed "The Anthracite Capital Of The World" in 1880. It was among the richest cities per capita on earth, the first American city to build a completely electric public trolley system, and served as a model for urban and corporate planning from the Atlantic to the Pacific. The city's architectural style was produced by some of the period's preeminent

Starting in the 1880s, southern and eastern European peasants replaced immigrants from western Europe and formed intensely ethnic neighborhoods within anthracite mining communities.

architects, such as Raymond Hood, who would later design Rockefeller Plaza in New York City.

Vaudeville found Scranton's socially and economically diverse population the perfect preview audience to perform before, and the city's red-light district was considered second to none. In part, this may have been because the mining industry drew an abundance of single males, as well as the fact that the region's renowned rail service made it easy to get to Scranton from anywhere.

As ground zero for J.P. Morgan's coal and rail cartel, northeastern Pennsylvania amassed tremendous wealth by 1900. Coal barons lived in American palaces, and stoutly defended the rights of private ownership, but then ignored those very rights in their efforts to force many independent mine operators out of business by controlling the cost of transporting their anthracite to market. Companies that survived such fixed shipping costs were often forced out for another reason—they paid a fair wage. When one mine operator was asked why he paid his workers so poorly, he responded, "They don't suffer. They can't even speak English."

The Scranton Times.

EXTRA.

Saturday's Circulation
21,550

33D YEAR—NO. 113.   10 PAGES—SCRANTON, PA., MONDAY AFTERNOON, MAY 12, 1902.—10 PAGES   ONE CENT A COPY

ALL MINES ARE IDLE.

Miners in the Entire Anthracite Field Have Obeyed the Order to Suspend Work Today===Electing Delegates to the Hazleton Convention.

SITUATION IN THE LOCAL COAL FIELD REVIEWED

New York, May 12.—There will be a meeting in this city tomorrow of the directors and presidents of some of the leading coal companies, at which the questions involved in the coal strike are expected to be discussed.

THE WYOMING VALLEY TIED UP.

THE SITUATION AT PITTSTON.

SCHUYLKILL REGION TIED UP.

HANNA STILL HOPEFUL.

ALL CLOSED AT SHAMOKIN.

MYSTERIOUS MESSAGES RECEIVED

Came From Philadelphia for "Chairman of Miners' Meetings" in Scranton.

BOTH WERE DELIVERED

CREMATING THE VICTIMS

Gathering in the Corpses at St. Pierre to Prevent a Pestilence.

SENDING RELIEF.

CLEMENCY FOR BOERS

Terms Offered by the British Are Likely to be Accepted.

LATEST REPORTS

SAYS BOERS WILL FIGHT.

THE PEACE NEGOTIATIONS.

FINANCIAL AND COMMERCIAL

Fine Fashionable HOSIERY

Of Exquisite Quality And Latest Designs.

My Ladies' Stockings...

A Valuable Object Lesson

Ladies' Superb Hosiery

Prices, $1.50, $2.00, $2.50 and $3.00 the pair.

Fine Lisle Thread Hosiery

$1.00

High Medium Grade Hosiery...

50c

Genuine Maco Yarn Hosiery...

25c

Bargains in Hosiery

15c

18c

"They" were the immigrants who came to America between 1881 and 1910 in what is called the "Atlantic Migration," a monumental dislocation of more than fourteen million people seeking to escape starvation, poverty, or political and religious repression. For them, the United States represented a promise of hope.

Assimilating ethnic and racial minorities has always challenged American society's underpinnings of equality. Immigrants found this society waiting for them on the docks of cities like Boston, Baltimore and New York. In 1900, New York City's population included more Italians than Rome, more Irish than Dublin, more Jews than Warsaw, and more blacks than any city in the world.

Jews entered the needle trades. Italians worked in construction trades. The Irish spoke the best English. Even as a minority, they became the most politically powerful. Tens of thousands of unskilled eastern and southern European immigrants speaking 20 languages settled in northeastern Pennsylvania, where coal companies offered low paying work in the anthracite mines.

Anglo-Saxon immigrants believed that new migrants were different than themselves, and publicly expressed an anti-Catholic, anti-immigration

Throughout this book, authentic images of front-page headlines from the Scranton Times chronicle some of the events associated with the Great Anthracite Coal Strike of 1902.

An example of an anthracite-burning stove used by many people in the northeastern United States to heat their homes and cook their meals.

sentiment which religious and political leadership failed to diffuse. By 1880, the Anglo-Saxon culture had become so entrenched in America that eastern and southern European immigrants got off the boat to discover their names being simplified. Italian immigrants who arrived in the U.S. "without papers" that identified them to immigration officials were referred to by the derogatory abbreviation "wops." The new immigrants were welcomed into the anthracite mining communities with bigotry and suspicion, which produced class-divided neighborhoods, like Irish Flats, Polish Hill, and Cheesetown.

By 1900, one-third of all anthracite workers were from eastern or southern Europe. Anglo-Saxon miners bemoaned that the immigrants depressed wages, and that anthracite mining had become a Russian and Polish occupation. Many left the region, skewing the ethnic diversity of

northeastern Pennsylvania again, this time toward the eastern European immigrants.

People from 26 countries migrated to northeastern Pennsylvania from the 1870's until immigration was curtailed by World War I. Yet a homogenous working class never evolved, as it had in Europe. The region remained divided by language, culture, and religion. Despite relentless hardships, however, these immigrants produced personal savings of over two million dollars in the northern field alone, and bought homes to raise families through which they would ultimately achieve their American dream.

Between 1893 and 1897, the United States experienced its third important economic depression of the 19th century. The federal government interpreted the unprecedented industrial expansion that occurred in the country after 1897 as a validation of America's free enterprise economy. However, the labor force that supported America's ascension as the world' most advanced industrial nation received almost nothing for its contribution.

By 1900, America had over thirty million workers, but no national enforcement of a minimum wage or a limit to hours worked. One million women were employed, but none worked in coal mining, owing to the rigorous nature of the work and miners' superstition. Women and girls endured their own industrial servitude in silk mills built near the anthracite region's larger towns.

Fewer than two million American workers

1825
Anthracite is used in a steam engine for the first time, but its intense heat destroys the grate.

1829
Anthracite mining begins in the Wyoming region.

1830
Europe abolishes serfdom and replaces collapsed empires with industrial capitalism. Great Britain's industrial revolution matures it into the "Workshop Of The World".

1833
A patent is awarded for using a hot air blast with anthracite coal to smelt iron ore.

1836
Anthracite is successfully employed to manufacture pig iron at the Valley Furnace near Pottsville.

THE DOUBT OF AN EARNEST, THOUGHTFUL, PATIENT AND LABORIOUS MIND IS WORTHY OF RESPECT. IN SUCH DOUBT MAY BE FOUND INDEED MORE FAITH THAN IN HALF THE CREEDS.

—Bishop John Lancaster Spaulding, *Means and Ends of Education*

were unionized nationally, and the press and the public generally viewed them as either a destabilizing criminal movement, or associated with the Socialist Party. At the turn of the century, the ideology and the politics of the Socialist Party differed dramatically from that of the Democratic and Republican parties, and offered working people and immigrants a distinct choice in thinking about the nature of government.

Democratic presidential candidate William Jennings Bryan railed at the Republican party's notion that J.P. Morgan, Andrew Carnegie and John Rockefeller were patriots. Eventually, though, socialism's dissatisfied liberalism conflicted with the prevailing political conservatism of early unions, and, like the U.S. government failed to advance the needs of the American worker. So the American worker went at it alone.

In 1886, the first significant labor organization in the United States was formed—the American Federation of Labor. It consisted of an alliance of different trade unions, like bricklayers, ironworkers and painters. However, coal mining was not considered a trade at this time, so mineworkers were not protected by AFL labor agreements. Bituminous miners in the Midwest began forming unions twenty five years earlier. By the time the AFL was created, bituminous miners had developed a collective bargaining organization that stabilized the soft coal mining industry across six states,

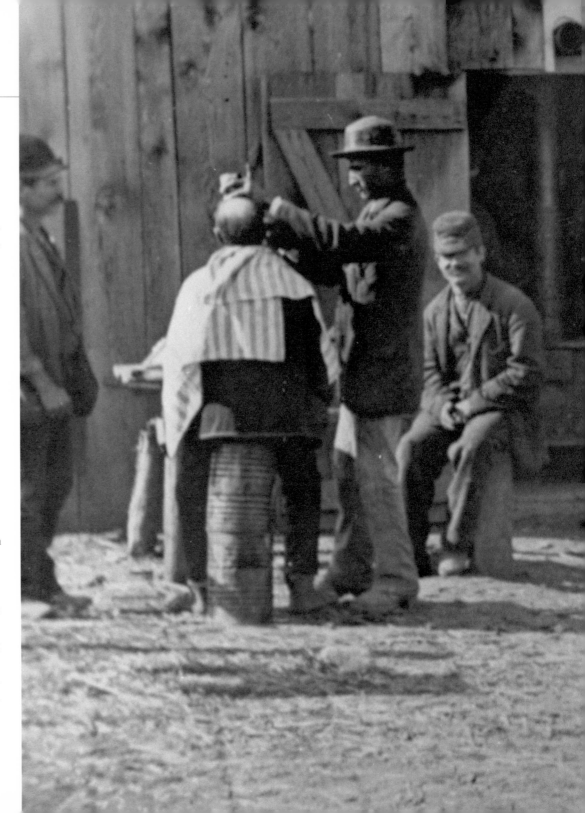

and resulted in a historic labor agreement based on peaceful negotiations and conciliation called the Interstate Joint Conference.

Anthracite miners also wanted a guaranteed set of work rights, but did not fare as well in their attempts to organize. John Siney's efforts to form an anthracite miner's union in Schuylkill County began in 1868, with the Workingmen's Benevolent Association.

The Workingmen's Benevolent Association initially secured higher wages for anthracite miners, and sparked other attempts to unify Anglo-Saxon miners into a legitimate and effective labor organization. However, language and ethnic divisions, the remoteness of anthracite towns, and ethnic bigotry all proved overwhelmingly difficult for labor organizers to overcome during this time.

One who tried was a woman named Mary Harris Jones, but she was better known as "Mother Jones", probably because her matronly appearance reminded the thousands of labor militants who came to hear her robust speeches of their own scolding but supportive mother. Mother Jones fearlessly appeared at all the great labor conflicts across the country, using her spry sense of humor and dramatic visage to galvanize public sympathy for the hardships of working men, women and children.

Before there was ever a World Series, baseball was already a popular athletic activity in the anthracite region.

SHORT STORIES FROM THE MINES

Some swore Mother Jones was a man wearing a dress. She said, "I have never had a vote and I have raised hell all over the is country! You don't need a vote to raise hell! You need convictions and a voice." Mother Jones personified the vigor felt in the hearts of the mining community. However, her tactics proved a better morale booster than effective labor strategy. It would be left to another noble warrior to transform idealism and commitment into a foundation for the anthracite miners that would create America's largest and most powerful industrial union.

Most of the immigrants who came to northeastern Pennsylvania arrived by train, and undoubtedly got their first glimpse of anthracite from the coal trains that passed them as they entered the region.

On A Wing And A Whiskey

Though they worked long hours, often six days a week, and had very little money, the immigrant miners and their families did have lives outside of the mines. Baseball was a popular activity in northeastern Pennsylvania at the turn of the century. Two of the most popular teams at that time were the Scranton Amateurs and the Pittston Brothers.

Ethnic churches were also very important in every faith throughout the anthracite region. The church was a place where the immigrants sought solace from miserable living and working conditions. It was also where they could share ideas and news. Most of these people could not read or write, so the only way they could communicate was through the spoken word.

In Lackawanna County alone in 1900 there were about 250 ethnically based churches. It is also estimated there were about 500 ethnically based saloons, which provided the miners with another means of recreation and communication.

Pennsylvania, Here I Come

The Welsh predominated the immigrants who settled in the anthracite region in the early 19th century. Their assimilation into northeastern Pennsylvania was easier than other cultures to follow. The area's countryside and weather was similar to what existed in south Wales. The Welsh also spoke English, and many had mining experience.

The Irish and Germans followed the Welsh, beginning in the 1830's and continuing through the Irish potato blight of the 1840's. The Irish came primarily to escape starvation and British repression over land ownership. By 1900, however, one-third of the anthracite work force—50,000 men—were either Slavic or Italian.

American steamship companies had hundreds of agents in eastern and southern Europe passing out circulars advertising that the Pennsylvania coal mines were paying laborers $35.00, compared to the $9.00 a month they would earn in Europe. By the last decade of the 19th century, though, for every hundred arriving immigrants, one-third would return to Europe because of economic or social difficulties.

Bryan's Song

The beginning of the 20th century was the coming of age of American labor. Business leaders thought labor unions had no business organizing their workers, and refused to believe a union could serve as a legitimate expression of their employee' desires. Politicians as well as labor leaders exploited this economic threat to working

people and immigrants to advance their own
political agendas.

William Jennings Bryan gave political voice
to Americans at this time who were beginning to
feel the need for social justice and who sensed
a growing corporate influence in government.
Between 1896 and 1910, he led the reformist
Democratic Party and had an important political
influence on Republican politicians such as
Theodore Roosevelt. Roosevelt came to believe
that if no executive action was taken to address
the American public's growing social and political uneasiness, William Jennings Bryan would
accuse him of kowtowing to financial interests
that controlled the Republican Party.

*Between 1896 and 1912, William Jennings Bryan was the
Democratic Party's presidential nominee three times, and
could have had the nomination for all five presidential elec-
tions during this period. He championed the values of the
agarian west and south against the economic policies favored
by most eastern banks and industrialists.*

KING COAL

The anthracite coal companies and anthracite railroads were the largest employers in northeastern Pennsylvania. They forged the region's economic foundation, and sustained the majority of its 750,000 residents. Among these combinations, the Philadelphia and Reading Railroad was the most powerful and most effective at regulating production to control the price of anthracite.

In 1897, it cost between $200,000 and $750,000 dollars to start up a colliery. Shafts had to be sunk and fitted with hoisting machinery, gangways had to be driven, chambers opened, engine houses built to power ventilation and pumping machinery, and mules and coal cars purchased.

On the surface, roads and slopes had to be graded, and machinery obtained to transport mined anthracite within the colliery. Mining was an expensive endeavor, and eliminating competition was one way to recover the capital investment in building and maintaining facilities, and in labor and equipment costs.

The cities of Pottsville, Wilkes-Barre, and Scranton became county seats and centers of coal production. Their industrial base expanded and helped maintain some economic autonomy from the influence of the coal and rail combination. It included mills, factories and locomotive repair shops, which lured entrepreneurs who established businesses that helped sustain outlying mining communities like Carbondale, Hazleton and Shamokin.

(Left) Labor activist Mother Jones visited Pennsylvania to support the interests of the miners and their families. (middle) Until the use of arbitration to resolve the Great Anthracite Coal Strike of 1902, U.S. presidents and governors employed the military to defend corporate property and assault picketing workers. (right) Every immigrant who came to northeastern Pennsylvania to work in the anthracite mines passed through this processing room at Ellis Island in New York harbor.

The Scranton Times.

EXTRA.   Yesterday's Circulation, 19,000

33D YEAR—NO. 181.   SCRANTON, PA., THURSDAY AFTERNOON, JULY 31, 1902.   ONE CENT A COPY

TROOPS CALLED OUT

The Eighth Regiment and the Governor's Troop Rushed to Shenandoah to Suppress Rioting----Twelfth Regiment Also Under Orders.

MINE LEADERS ASSIST IN SUPPRESSING THE DISORDER

JOSEPH BEDDELL IS STILL ALIVE

NEGRO LYNCHED BY ANGRY MOB

DEPUTY SHOT BY A STRIKER

MOB SURROUNDS A TROLLEY CAR

Another Batch of New Bargains

Will await your attention tomorrow morning. The goods offered are all of the better class and when seen by buyers of discrimination and good taste, are sure to be picked up quickly.

The Shirt

ANTHRACITE HISTORICAL TIMELINE

1840

Anthracite's use to smelt iron ore is perfected. The advancement of the closed-grate heating system promotes anthracite as a home heating fuel.

1846

Eastern Pennsylvania's canal system expands to 643 miles, thus substantially lowering the cost of delivering anthracite from a mine to a market.

1848

Anthracite miners in Schuylkill County form the Bates Union, the first recorded American coal union.

1860

Anthracite is firmly established as an important industrial and domestic fuel.

1864

The Bessemer process initiates America's industrial advancement out of the Iron Age and into the Steel Age.

THE MOST BEAUTIFUL SIGHT THAT WE SEE IS THE CHILD AT LABOR;
AS EARLY AS HE MAY GET AT LABOR THE MORE BEAUTIFUL, THE MORE
USEFUL DOES HIS LIFE GET TO BE. —Asa G. Chandler, founder of Coca-Cola

CHAPTER 3

By 1890, thirty years of labor organizing in the bituminous fields resulted in the formation of the United Mine Workers of America. The UMWA's goal was to amass the centrally organized collective bargaining power needed to achieve fair wages and safe working conditions for all coal industry workers in its 18 districts nationally. However, this solidarity would come at a cost.

In 1898, 11 miners were killed and 35 wounded in Virden, Illinois, by state militia protecting African-Americans imported to replace striking bituminous miners. By now no stranger to the belligerent tendencies of the coal operators, or its own membership, the union dispatched its energetic 28-year-old national vice-president, John Mitchell, to attend to the families of the dead miners. Mitchell had worked in the bituminous mines in Illinois beginning at age 12, and became passionately committed to vanquishing the working and living conditions that he believed stole his childhood.

The poorest and most ethnically intense neighborhood within a company town was known as "The Patch."

When John Mitchell assumed the presidency of the UMWA in 1899, the union had been trying to organize the miners in the anthracite fields for four years, and there were less than 30,000 members nationally. In the following four years, national membership increased to 300,000, and almost half of those miners worked in the anthracite districts.

John Mitchell persuaded membership to curtail violent reprisals, and employers to embrace the stability that trade agreements provided them. These labor pacts increased productivity as well as wages, reduced hours worked, and successfully addressed health and safety issues for bituminous and anthracite coal miners. Mitchell would eventually build the United Mine Workers of America into the country's first nationally powerful industrial union and its largest collective bargaining labor organization.

In 1900, the poverty line in industrial sections of the United States for a family of five was about $460.00 a year. Most miners struggled to make even that. Some operators calculated wages based on what was called the "equilibrium of empty bellies"—just enough pay to sustain the miner

and raise the next generation of mine workers. Operators also hired non-English speaking immigrants to work as laborers, to maintain a tension between skilled and unskilled workers along ethnic lines that diluted any enthusiasm for joining the UMWA.

Anthracite mining was an unusual blend of physical strength, technical skills, teamwork, leadership, discipline and courage. Most of those who worked underground worked essentially on their own. The labyrinth of gangways and the distance from company managers made supervision impractical, and instigated a self-reliant disposition in these men that served as the fuse for UMWA organizers.

It is estimated that these miners extracted more than one billion tons of anthracite coal from northeastern Pennsylvania between 1800 and 1920. Enough anthracite was mined underneath a 25 square mile area of the city of Scranton alone by 1912 to fill almost the entire Panama Canal.

However, this prosperity came at a remarkable cost. Between 1869 and 1897, more than seven thousand men and boys were killed in anthracite mines. Almost 18,000 were disabled—twice the rate

(left) The immigrant anthracite miners and their families would affectionately call John Mitchell "Johnny D'Mitch." (right) A group of boys employed in a colliery wait for the paymaster on payday.

of bituminous mining. It could be calculated that for every day between the day the Statue of Liberty was dedicated in New York harbor in 1886, and America's entry into World War One in 1917, one man or boy working in an anthracite colliery would lose his life.

Though state mine inspectors found independent operators violated safety codes more frequently than the larger coal companies, they just as often reported that miners were at fault in accidents, and cited ignored safety rules or short cuts as causes of many fatalities. Yet miners were literally

between a rock and a hard place. The more time spent setting timbers—called "dead work" because miners were not paid for shoring their work place—the less coal a miner sent to the surface, and the less he earned.

The chambers in which the miners extracted the anthracite from were almost completely dark. There were no lights underground, except a coal oil lamp affixed to the miner's headgear. It had a small wick that provided about as much light as one birthday candle. Visibility extended no more than two or three feet in any direction.

COMING GENERATIONS WILL LEARN EQUALITY FROM POVERTY, AND LOVE FROM WOES. —Kahlil Gibran, *A Handful of Sand on the Shore*

The mines could also be damp. Bad drainage created frequent standing water. Rats were prevalent. Hundreds would run throughout a mine, but underground tenderfoots were warned to never kill a mine rat. They could detect a fall, or gas. If they scrambled up a tunnel, you better too.

Working in the anthracite mines was described by miners as "dying by inches," sapping them of spirit and health. There, as a miner's legend had it, death waited to blow out his lamp. Most miners were haunted to their graves by debilitating respiratory diseases caused by breathing dust and powder smoke. Their hearing became diminished from the stunted echoes of underground explosions. Their skin would become permanently mottled with fine coal dust. Many miners developed chronic posture problems from interminable bending from working in chambers only three to five feet high.

(below) A breaker was a part of a "colliery," which is the term that encompasses a coal mine's entire physical plant. (right) A common scene inside an anthracite breaker a hundred years ago. The "cracker boss" stood among the breaker boys to insure they kept to their work of cleaning rock from the anthracite coal.

DICKSON COLLIERY
1886

A miner's eyes burned in the faint light of a coal mine. His chamber would become thick with coal-dust, like black snow. It could suddenly fill with asphyxiating, heavier gases at the floor and lighter, explosive gases at the ceiling. Firedamp, or carbonated hydrogen, made the miner's lamp burn bluish, and was explosive. It pressed heavily on their eyelids, and stuck their eyelashes together. Black damp-carbonic acid-produced a quiet, painless death compared to the disfiguring, unforeseen demise caused by cave-ins, blasting, or machinery.

The Industrial Revolution transformed Western Europe and the United States from an agrarian to an industrial society, and child labor was used extensively. America entered the 20th century afflicted by an epidemic of child labor: in the retail stores and sweatshops of its growing cities, in eastern textile mills and glass factories, in Gulf Coast canaries.

Most Americans at the turn of the century were unaware of this situation. Federal and state

(left) Fatality rates for mining anthracite coal at the turn of the century exceeded six deaths per 1000 miners annually. Comparatively, fatality rates in mines in Germany were three per thousand, 1.5 per thousand in Belgium and 1 per thousand in France and Britain. (right) Another scene inside an anthracite breaker where the "cracker boss" made sure the breaker boys kept to their work of cleaning rock.

government kept few child labor records, and enacted no enforceable age or workplace legislation. It was left mostly to communities to determine how they would protect their children, but many felt working children kept families off public charity. Asa G. Chandler, the founder of Coca-Cola, once said, "The most beautiful sight that we see is the child at labor; as early as he may get at labor the more beautiful, the more useful does his life get to be."

In 1890, nearly 20 percent of the anthracite labor force was under sixteen years of age. Operators wanted cheap labor; families were desperate for money. Teenage boys performed some of the most dangerous underground jobs. Most boys in mining communities around 1900 left school by their 12th birthday to help support their families. Their first job working in a colliery would be picking boney while straddling an endless and mesmerizing roar and blur of anthracite passing through the breaker.

Until washeries became common in processing coal, breaker boys protected themselves from the dusty and noisy conditions by breathing through neckerchiefs, chewing tobacco and plugging their ears with wads of clay or string. Their fingers were relentlessly cut from sticking their hands in chutes picking rock from the coal. New boys learned that their fingers healed faster if they urinated on them.

It was the Cracker Boss's job to keep the boys productive. He used an oak switch to motivate them. There was no protection from that. His job was to make sure that the boys' time was well used from the point of view of the company.

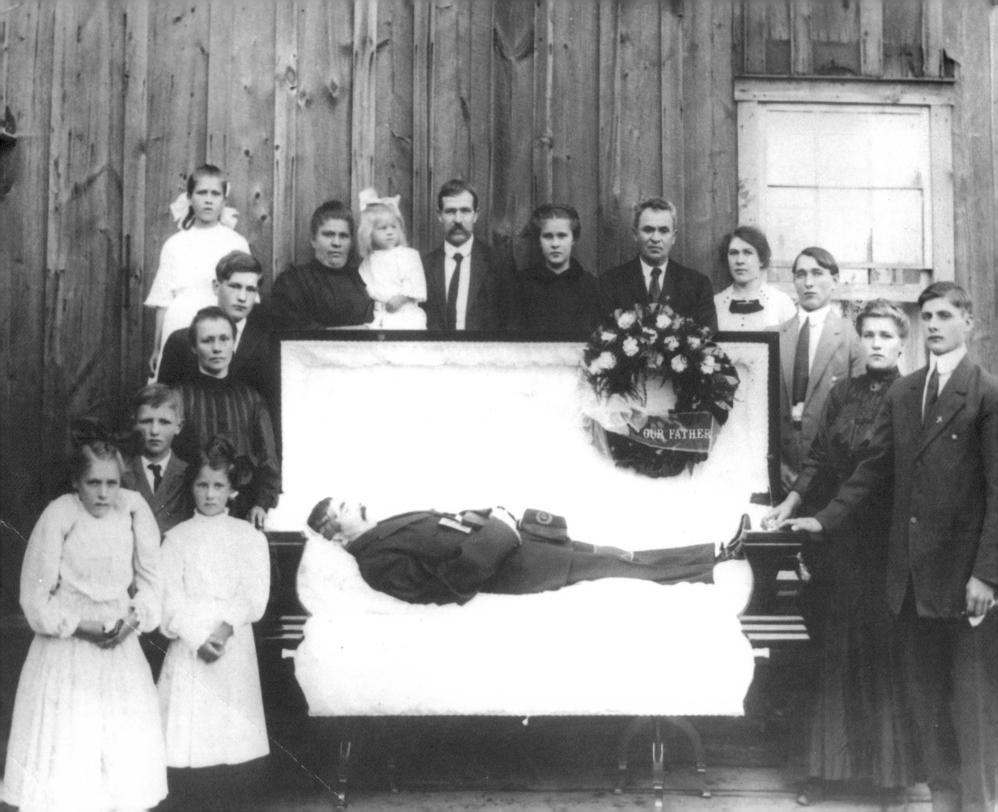

The Cracker Boss would clobber a kid if he fell asleep, or if he began to see slate finding its way into the bin where only coal should be.

Breaker boys around 1900 made a salary of about a dollar fifty a week, or two to three cents an hour. Though this was a practical pittance, it was so important to the family. It meant, however, that a boy's childhood was truncated very early.

John Mitchell said of the breaker boys, "They reminded me of the misery of my childhood. They have the bodies and faces of boys, but came to meetings where I spoke and stood as still as men and listened to every word. I was amazed as I saw those eager eyes peering at me from little eager faces. I felt I was fighting for innocent childhood. The fight had new meaning for me."

Death and accident rates were higher in anthracite mining than in bituminous mining, and child labor more prevalent. Some large mining companies provided employees and families with free medical care. Some companies offered assistance if injuries were severe, like a losing an eye or a leg. A few anthracite companies provided benefit funds, though miners knew this was only to entice them from joining the union. The majority of operators felt accident benefits were a luxury, and ignored victims or deducted medical costs from wages for treating influenza and tuberculosis. Miners had no choice in treatments or doctors. Most community assistance was reserved for victims of disasters, like fires and cave-ins.

Mining accidents were torturous for a community. Fearful family members knew the men were trapped right under their feet, only it was impossible to get to them. Residents stormed a colliery when it heard "the three shorts", three sharp blasts of the breaker whistle that signaled an accident. Families rarely filed damage suits, although the courts held the state was financially responsible for anthracite accidents, and not the coal companies. Some companies offered survivors a hundred dollars and a return ticket to the old country.

Some operators built churches, and gave free coal to hospitals and railroad passes to charitable organizations. They also built company towns. Houses were small, and offered no privacy. They were made of hickory, which was available and cheap because it attracted bedbugs. Some homes had dirt floors, and walls stuffed with rags for insulation. Residents of company towns had no tenant rights. No guests were permitted. Fourth amendment search and seizure protection was ignored. Many operators set local tax rates, and managed, or ignored, environmental protection and public services like water and sanitation. Miners were discouraged or prohibited from living elsewhere.

Company towns were frequently remote outposts of civilization, so the mine owners built

1870

A relief plan established by the Philadelphia & Reading Coal & Iron Company pays a miner's widow $30 for funeral expenses, $3 per week, and $1 per week for every child younger than 12 years old.

1872

Franklin Gowen forms the first consortium of coal carriers to control shipping costs.

1875

The bituminous product "coke" replaces anthracite in making pig iron. This market loss compels anthracite mine owners to produce coal in a finer grade called "domestic".

1877

The eventual execution of 20 suspected Molly Maguires brings this violent chapter of anthracite history to a close.

1877

A railroad strike in Pittsburgh inspires a riot that causes millions of dollars in damage to the Pennsylvania Railroad and provokes middle-class sympathy for railroad companies.

| EXTRA. | # The Scranton Times. | Yesterday's Circulation, 22,200 |

33D YEAR—NO. 251.   10 PAGES—SCRANTON, PA., TUESDAY AFTERNOON, OCTOBER 21, 1902.—10 PAGES   ONE CENT A COPY.

STRIKE IS TODAY OFFICIALLY DECLARED OFF

Miners in Convention at Wilkes Barre Accept Arbitration and Will Return to Work on Next Thursday.

THERE WAS NOT A DISSENTING VOTE.

Wilkes-Barre, Oct. 21---The strike is ended. Delegates representing the army of mine workers in the anthracite fields by their action taken in convention this morning, formally declared the strike off, and ordered the 147,000 mine workers back to the breakers and the mines. The dictation of the convention is that work be resumed on Thursday next.

By the unanimous adoption of the report of the resolution committee the convention at noon made it publicly known that the mine workers favored the plan of arbitration and that they were willing to return to work while the arbitration commission investigates the conditions in the coal fields which provoked the strike and its continuance for nearly six months. By the action taken they make it manifest that they are satisfied to abide by the finding of the commission appointed by the president of the United States.

Wilkes-Barre, Sept. 21—Secretary Wilson and the resolution committee entered the convention hall at 10.45 o'clock and found the convention in session and waiting for the report of the committee. It was read by Mr. Wilson. The great interest which centered in the report was manifest by the death-like silence which prevailed during the reading of the recommendations of the committee. There was not a sound in the hall save that of the national secretary's voice, and everybody strained their ears so as to catch every word of the report.

The resolution was addressed to President Roosevelt and recommended that the mine workers return to work on Thursday. It was adopted and by its adoption the great strike was formally declared off.

The Resolution Adopted.

Following is the resolution:

We, the committee on resolutions, beg leave to recommend that the following communication be adopted and forwarded to Theodore Roosevelt, President of the United States:

Hon. Theodore Roosevelt, President of the United States, Washington, D. C.

Dear Sir:—We, the representatives of the employes of the various coal companies engaged in operating mines in the anthracite coal fields of Pennsylvania, in convention assembled, having under consideration your telegram of October 15, sent to John Mitchell, president of the United Mine Workers of America, which reads as follows: "I have appointed as a commission, Brigadier General John M. Wilson, Mr. E. W. Parker, Judge George Gray, Mr. E. E. Clarke, Mr. Thomas H. Watkins and Bishop John L. Spaulding, with Hon. Carroll D. Wright as recorder. These men are acceptable to the operators and I now most earnestly ask and urge that the miners likewise accept this commission. It is a matter of vital concern to all our people and especially to those in our great cities who are least well off, that the mining of coal should be resumed without a day's unnecessary delay."

We have decided to accept the proposition herein embodied and submit all questions at issue between the operators and the mine workers of the anthracite coal region for adjustment to the commission which you have named. In pursuance of that decision we shall report for work on Thursday morning, October 23, in the positions and working places occupied by us prior to the inauguration of the strike.

discussion afresh on the question of the men returning to work. One delegate declared that in previous strike the Lehigh Coal company had declared they would not take the strikers in their places and two months after the strike was off, the men were all back in their places. There were cries of "question," showing that the delegates were anxious to settle the question. President Mitchell, however, declared that until the last man had been heard the vote would not be taken. Secretary Wilson, at this point, took occasion to make a speech in favor of adopting the recommendations. He said that the miners has won a victory and that the original demands of the miners for arbitration had been acceded to and he could not understand why some men were still hanging out.

CONVENTION ADJOURNS.

President Mitchell then asked the press to state for him that all engineers, firemen, pumpmen, foremen, stable bosses, railroad men and all those classes of special labor necessary in getting the machinery in order for work, shall return to work tomorrow morning. The convention sang "America," and adjourned.

ANTICIPATING THE RESULT.

Secretary Wilson said that it appeared that several of the delegates were anticipating what would be done regarding their places if they returned to work. If the strikers found that they could not get back, it would be a matter for the arbitration commission. He said:

"You have, by your conduct of this strike, won the respect and confidence of the American people. If you turn down this proposition made by the president of the United States, do you think you can retain the confidence of the people who have helped you? You have won the victory and you should accept it."

Several delegates were heard, and a delegate asked that in view of the numerous foreigners among the delegates that they have the proposition explained to them in their tongue. Speeches of explanation then were made in Lithuanian, Slavish and Polish.

While the foreign explanations were in progress the Slavish speaker was interrupted by a delegate, and the speaker turned to Mr. Mitchell and said:

"He wants to know how much he

JOHN MITCHELL.

NEWS PLEASES THE OPERATORS

ALL TRAINS ON THE RAILROADS WILL GIVE WAY TO THE SHIPMENT OF COAL

MARKLE WOULD NOT TALK

New York, Oct. 21—The coal operators assembled for their regular Tuesday meeting today, when the news of the settlement of the coal strike by the Wilkes-Barre convention reached them. "I am very glad to hear of it," said President Baer. "Coal will now be rushed to market on the jump."

"The first mined ought to be here by the last of the week," said President Truesdale.

"I expected this result. Work will be rushed," said President Fowler.

"Hardly necessary to say I am pleased. Everything will give way on our road to coal trains," said President Olyphant.

"More than pleased," said Chairman Thomas.

"Our line will get coal to market as soon as possible," said Vice-President Fayre, of the Lehigh.

John Markle, of the Independents, declined to discuss the matter.

The Rev. Father Curran was called upon for a speech. He said that this was the happiest day of his life as it was the day of a glorious victory of labor and organized labor throughout the world. Father Curran exhorted the men to stand by their union and their leaders.

The President's Reply To Miners

Washington, Oct. 21—The following reply was sent to the miners' convention:

"Upon receipt of your telegram of this date, the president summoned the commission to meet here on Friday next, the 24 inst, at 10 a. m.

(Signed), O. B. CORTELYOU, Secretary to the President.

CONVENTION OF IRISH LEAGUE

Boston, Oct. 21—A notable gathering of leaders of international reputation made remarkable the opening of the first convention of the United Irish League in this city yesterday. John F. Redmond, M. P., Michael Davitt and John Dillon, M. P., envoys from Ireland; Hon. Edward Blake, Irish M. P., ex-United States Senator Smith, of New Jersey, Patrick Egan, former United States minister to Chili, and Patrick Ford, of the Irish World, were among the delegates.

Hon. Bourke Cochran was made temporary chairman. Addressing the convention, Mr. Cockran said that an appeal to arms by the Irish people would be folly, rather than patriotism, but that when the truth of the Irish question should become apparent to the world, an adjustment of the difficulty would be possible.

The committee on credentials reported 342 delegates present, including 173 delegates at large, representing 13 states, the District of Columbia, and Canada.

The convention then organized with John F. Finnerty, of Chicago, as permanent chairman. Committees were appointed with the following chairmen:

Rules, General O'Beirne, New York; by-laws, M. P. Curran, Massachusetts; platform and resolutions, M. J. Ryan, Philadelphia; ways and means, United States Senator Smith, New Jersey; permanent organization, Patrick Ford, of New York.

The evening session was wildly enthusiastic, especially during the speeches of John Dillon and Michael Davitt, and the resolutions which were adopted at the close of the session were adopted amid cheers.

A number of letters of regret were read, notably from President Roosevelt, Governor Crane, Mayor Collins and Bishop Conaty.

CARDINAL TO CALL A MEETING

this country is not sufficiently well established to cut itself away from the direction of the propaganda. It is also argued by the advocates of the present condition that, as foreigners by birth still dominate in the affairs of the Catholic church in this country, it would be injudicious and hasty to establish an American church from heterogeneous elements, which would be American in name only.

We can't say more than that, and the excellence of our stock fully warrants the statement.

PISTOL DUEL ON THE STREET.

Paint Lick, Ky., Oct. 21—Dr. Edwin F. Poynts and John Siler engaged in a pistol duel on the street here last evening. Bystanders say from eight to twelve shots were exchanged and when the smoke cleared away, it was found that both men had sustained serious wounds. Poynts was shot through the left wrist, the right arm and on the left side in the region of the kidneys. The physicians consider the latter wound dangerous.

Siler received dangerous wounds and his condition is critical. Siler had recently taken charge of the hotel at this place, where Dr. Poynts had boarded with the former proprietor. Siler accused Poynts of talking about him and taking treats away from his hotel. The men met last night and after midnight and after exchanging a few words began firing with the above result.

FINANCIAL AND COMMERCIAL.

New York, Oct. 21—The stock market opened rather less active than in the final quarter of an hour last night. Prices were slightly lower, but were much better than the London figures. A considerable number of international list, including the Baltimore and Ohio, Canadian Pacific and Pennsylvania were 3⁄8 lower. Norfolk and Western was 3⁄8 higher in spite of the 6 per cent. loss in London. Leading stocks in the industrials were firm, notable the steel stocks, Sugar and Amalgamated Copper were steady.

The following quotations are furnish'd The Times by Haight & Freese Co., 316-315 Mears building; W. D. Runyon, manager.

stores to sell provisions that the miner and his family needed to subsist. Prices in company stores could run as high as 40 to 50 percent higher than at a regular retail store. Some operators prohibited miners from patronizing local stores by paying wages in a company-issued currency called "scrip." However, the company store extended credit to the miners, which they could not get anywhere else.

The large companies ultimately discontinued company stores by World War One. Until this time, though, miners would be cashless, pensionless occupational prisoners. Their warden was a lack of education or money. These immigrants believed their fate was a test of endurance by God. And as the region's priests celebrated Sunday mass, the rumble they heard was more than empty bellies. It was the coming industrial war.

(left) The United Mine Workers of America made its headquarters for the 1900 strike in Hazleton. For the 1902 strike, John Mitchell based the union at the Hotel Hart in Wilkes-Barre, where he signed the resolution to end the strike. (right) The Westmoreland Breaker typifies the design of a coal processing building. Mine cars filled with anthracite would be pulled up a wooden ramp and dumped into the breaker at the top of the building. The coal would then slide down wood chutes, and young boys would pick out the rock from the coal and sort it by size for further processing. Workers could tell what time it was by how the sunlight that entered through the windows was captured by intense dust inside the building.

SHORT STORIES FROM THE MINES

What is a Breaker?

When mine cars loaded with anthracite reached daylight, they went to the "tipple," where the coal was dumped into a giant building called the breaker. There were hundreds of breakers throughout northeastern Pennsylvania, rising above the terrain like cheerless sentries prevailing over the lives of the families living in their shadow. Here anthracite coal was separated from rock, called "boney," and sorted by size.

Processing the mined coal and making it usable for different applications was an entirely separate industrial process than mining it. Breakers were the most visible part of the preparation plant. Some were 15 stories tall, and the sound of the coal being pulverized into different sizes could be heard from far away. Workers inside the breakers could tell time by how the shafts of sunlight captured by the intense coal dust moved across the various processing rooms.

Breakers were extremely noisy, dirty and dangerous environments. Ironically, young boys and old-timers no longer able to work underground worked in them.

How Does a Green Plant Become a Black Mineral?

Simply put, all varieties of coal formed from the plant debris of prehistoric jungle growth. Centuries before the dinosaurs, giant ferns were an abundant type of vegetable life in Pennsylvania. They could commonly grow as big as pine trees.

This debris turned ancient swamps into immense bogs, which ultimately became submerged beneath increasing layers of debris. Over millions and millions of years, this sediment formed a kind of lid of such a colossal weight and thickness that no air could reach the buried bogs. Heat and pressure from the earth's biochemical and geochemical processes "cooked" the bogs into coal.

A coal vein one foot thick required five to eight feet of plant debris. Many jungles would have had to grow, die, fall, decay, and rise again to produce this thick a deposit. The so-called Mammoth Vein near Tamaqua was an extraordinary 114 feet thick.

(left) Coal companies issued their own currency to their employees to discourage the use of non-company stores for purchasing provisions such as food and mining supplies. (above) The immigrants brought their strong faith in God with them from the Old Country. Churches became the center for sharing news because parishioners spoke the same language. (right) A butcher shop such as this, well supplied with fresh meats, would not accept "scrip," and was therefore unavailable to miners who were paid in this currency.

Risky Business

In 1901 alone, 513 anthracite workers were killed on the job, 441 of those miners. Almost half of these deaths were from rock falls that crushed, asphyxiated, or caused fatal catastrophic injuries.

Things were only a little less dangerous above ground. In 1901, the anthracite industry employed almost 150,000 people. A third of those worked in surface jobs, where other opportunities existed for a worker to be killed or maimed. Superintendents, bookkeepers and clerks staffed the offices. Foremen roamed the breaker, tipple, washery, shunting tracks, machine shop and pump and ventilation rooms, supervising blacksmiths, carpenters, engineers, machinists, weighmasters, timberers, and slate pickers.

These workers were mostly salaried, earning about two hundred to four hundred dollars a year. When a colliery was operating, everyone worked six days a week. Some, like firemen and pumpmen, worked seven. Some of the larger operations processed more than 700 coal cars every day during peak production periods.

Drilling augers like the one this miner is using to bore a powder hole commonly weighed over 80 pounds.

THE BOY PRESIDENT

John Mitchell was born in an impoverished coal town in Illinois in 1870. His mother died when he was 2. His father remarried, but was killed when Mitchell was 6. His stepmother, who consistantly abused him, raised Mitchell and his four brothers and sisters.

Mitchell quit school in the 5th grade, and ran away from home at ten. At 12, he began working as a trapper boy in a bituminous mine. He sat in complete darkness every day opening and shutting wooden doors in the tunnels.

He became a union man early, and proved to be dedicated to the principles of the United Mine

Workers of America. By the time Mitchell was 29, he was elected president of the UMWA on his own merit. Since then, no one close to Mitchell's youth has assumed leadership of a national union.

John Mitchell was intensely concerned with public opinion. He believed labor should reach out beyond the working class and represent a cross-class concern to influence public opinion and political leadership. Consequently, Mitchell constructed a conservative strategy for the UMWA, one that annoyed some in the union and led to a contentiousness that finally removed him from control in 1908.

(left) To support his efforts in organizing the immigrant miners throughout the anthracite region, John Mitchell would associate himself with the Catholic Church, despite the church's general feeling that labor unions were not desirable because they perpetrated violence and criminal activities. In this photograph, Mitchell is seen with Bishop Michael J. Hoban of the Scranton Diocese, and President Theodore Roosevelt, during a visit by the Chief Executive to northeastern Pennsylvania in 1908. (right) The anthracite region evolved into a predominately Catholic community, and priests were revered figures in the eyes of the immigrants. (right) Father John J. Curran was held in high esteem outside of the immigrant population as well, and became a confidant to Theodore Roosevelt.

THE RIGHTS AND INTERESTS OF THE LABORING MAN WOULD BE
PROTECTED AND CARED FOR NOT BY LABOR AGITATORS, BUT BY
CHRISTIAN MEN TO WHOM GOD IN HIS INFINITE WISDOM HAS
GIVEN CONTROL OF THE PROPERTY INTERESTS OF THE COUNTRY.
—George Baer, railroad president

CHAPTER 4

The massive influx of immigrants into American society as it entered the 20th century helped Catholicism become America's largest organized religion, with over eight million worshipers. John Mitchell sensed an alliance with the Catholic Church might be a catalyst to unionize the 150,000 immigrants working in the anthracite mines. By preaching the gospel of the trade agreement instead of the use of violence as a way for both labor and capital to achieve stability and prosperity in northeastern Pennsylvania, he became a friend with Scranton's bishop, Michael J. Hoban. Through this relationship, Mitchell finally connected with the immigrant workers, something no labor leader at the time had ever achieved, or even tried.

In spite of wretched working and living conditions that in many instances exceeded the hardship of southern slaves, Bishop Hoban inspired his tumultuous flock with intelligence and humility.

The Delaware, Lackawanna and Western railroad yards in Scranton, Pennsylvania, about 100 years ago. Today, this site is preserved as a national historic site dedicated to the history of the anthracite railroads.

He reminded them that their family bonds and faith in God were sources of salvation. Under his guidance, the church expanded its presence throughout the Dioceses' 11 counties. It opened night schools for the breaker boys, and created religious orders for ethnic women.

Mitchell secured another tactical resource and lifelong friend in Father John J. Curran, pastor of St. Mary's Church, Wilkes-Barre's largest Catholic parish. Curran was an ex-breaker boy, and an unfailing miner's champion who was also respected by northeastern Pennsylvania's industrialists. Curran served as a reliable source for press reports about the labor struggles, and would become such an essential envoy between labor and capital in the region that Theodore Roosevelt counted him among his most trusted advisors in the country.

The immigrants revered their priests as no others in the coalfields. When they saw the bond that their bishop and the most well known priest in the Wyoming and Lackawanna Valleys had with John Mitchell, they flocked to UMWA rallies. Between 1898 and 1900, these people elevated John Mitchell in their lives to near sainthood.

His picture hung in homes throughout the region, next to icons of their patron saints. As President of the United Mine Workers of America in 1900, he was even more well known in the anthracite region than the President of the United States, William McKinley. The anthracite miners would designate every October 29th "John Mitchell Day." And in 1919, they would bring John Mitchell back to northeastern Pennsylvania, to bury him in Cathedral Cemetery.

Northeastern Pennsylvania's churches framed the rich folk imagination of the anthracite communities. Anthracite songs recall the colorful immigrant atmosphere of the hard coal region, and were composed in sweat and blood to convey feelings and fears, and heartaches and hopes. Miners and their families restored themselves with music, dance, homemade wine, and "Polinky"— a concoction of beer, whiskey and red pepper, blended in a washtub with a broom handle, and enjoyed from a tin cup.

Anthracite mining surpassed its role as the immigrant's economic sustenance, to dominate their lives and escalate labor's intractable connection with class warfare out of the mine pits

A Coal and Iron Policeman armed with a Winchester rifle, probably provided by the coal and railroad companies and the type of gun employed by the security force to kill 19 immigrant miners during the Lattimer Massacre in 1897.

George Baer was J.P. Morgan's eyes and ears in the anthracite coal fields, where anthracite's extraordinary geographic concentration there compelled Morgan to invest in the railroads. Morgan would eventually own 91% of the coal shipping industry in northeastern Pennsylvania.

and into the melting pot. John Mitchell instilled in this revolution an evolution of non-violence, and legitimized America's labor movement.

Widespread violence in the anthracite fields' southern counties was frequently front-page news after the Civil War. A secret society of Irish immigrants there called the Molly Maguires was accused of waging a civil war of intimidation and revenge against coal company officials. Coal and rail operators, politicians, and pro-railroad newspapers blamed the terrorism on labor unions, to fuel an anti-labor sentiment in a public already in fear for its life.

Beginning in 1876, this societal persecution became a legal prosecution. The investigations, trials and executions of twenty accused members of the Molly Maguires for murders occurring

between 1862 and 1875 were carried out entirely by allies of the anthracite railroad and mining companies. The state supplied only the courtroom and gallows. In actuality, the violence revealed the need for a legitimate labor union to represent miners in circumstances of discrimination and oppression

Whether or not the Irish immigrants were guilty or innocent of murder, their executions were a warning to America that big business had become so powerful it could supersede the constitution. The country's next warning would come twenty one years later, in 1897, in a place called Lattimer.

On September 10th, 1897, about 300 non-union Polish and Hungarian mine workers set out from the Harwood Colliery near Hazleton to encourage mine employees at the colliery at Lattimer to join their walkout. Independent mines began to be being taxed for employing immigrants, and these mine owners began to deduct this tax from the wages of the immigrants themselves. This wage reduction, combined with pugnacious treatment by mine superintendents, drove the immigrant workers to the breaking point.

Coal operators called the miners' parade illegal, and asked for protection from Luzerne County Sheriff James Martin, a former mine foreman. As the marchers neared the mine at Lattimer later that afternoon, they were confronted by Martin and a picket line of over a hundred somber Coal

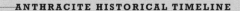
1880's
A labor organization called Workers International is established in England.

1885
The Anthracite Mining Act resurrects earlier mine safety regulations, but fails to reduce accidents.

1886
The Statue Of Liberty is completed.

1887
Steam and electric locomotives begin to replace mules in larger underground gangways.

1888
In Shenandoah, the Coal and Iron Police break a strike by shooting numerous miners picketing against strikebreakers.

NEVER BELIEVE THAT A FEW CARING PEOPLE CAN'T CHANGE THE WORLD. FOR, INDEED, THAT'S ALL WHO EVER HAVE.

—Margaret Mead

and Iron Policemen sighting down coal company issued Winchester rifles. As the Sheriff attempted to stop the march, he drew his pistol and pulled the trigger, but his gun failed to fire. The immigrants were not as lucky with the Winchesters. More than a hundred rounds were fired by the deputies, killing eight and hitting more than 40, some in the back as they ran for safety. As the sun set, the death count rose to 19, and news of the Lattimer Massacre spread throughout the region, and the country. The New York Times carried the story the next day on its front page.

Pennsylvania's governor dispatched 2500 national guardsmen the following morning to contain the community's cry for justice. Sheriff

Martin and 73 deputies were arrested and charged with murder. A coroner's investigation determined the killings were avoidable. The strike continued throughout a five-week trial, and swelled to 11,000 miners when the district attorney's inept prosecution helped to return not guilty verdicts for Sheriff Martin and every deputy.

The Lattimer Massacre provided the United Mine Workers exactly the turning point it needed to unite ethnic and Anglo-Saxon mine workers. It inspired in them a common identity based on their occupation. By August of 1899, UMWA membership in the anthracite region swelled from 7,000 to 90,000, and compelled John Mitchell to make his first visit there. Publicly, he rallied the

anthracite workers to exploit their long sought solidarity and eradicate two generations of industrial servitude in northeastern Pennsylvania. Privately, he thought the majority Republican Party would not allow labor unrest to become a campaign issue for the democratic candidate, William Jennings Bryan, in the 1900 presidential election.

One hundred twenty-five thousand miners walked out of the collieries in the strike of 1900, shutting down the industry for 43 days, and launching the United States into a century of profound, heroic change. Republican politicians ultimately did intercede to compel coal and rail operators to agree to a wage increase, the miners' first in twenty years.

John Mitchell was considered the leader of America's labor movement. However, the agreement with the mine operators had no expiration date, and did not address important living and working conditions. And the coal and rail operators still refused to recognize the United Mine Workers of America as anthracite labor's collective bargaining agent. In their relentless conflict with the industrialists, the miners won the 20th century's first round. The fight, though, was far from over.

The Philadelphia & Reading Railroad became anthracite's biggest mining and shipping operation. George F. Baer, a Civil War veteran groomed by J.P. Morgan to organize all anthracite operations into an economic juggernaut that defined coal

policy in the United States, ran it. Baer became the defiant voice and the uncompromising face of the anthracite trust. His philosophy was brutally simple. In a telegram to John Mitchell, Baer once wrote, "Anthracite mining is a business, and not a religious, sentimental, or academic proposition." For George Baer, there was no comparison between the property rights of the corporations and the human rights of mine workers. Though fierce competition among the railroads continually crippled the industry, they were even more ferociously united behind Baer's "mob rule" vision of the United Mine Workers of America.

John Mitchell would use the unaddressed issues of union recognition and working conditions as justification for pursuing a new contract with the operators at the beginning of 1901, despite personal fears of launching another strike in hard coal country. Rumors of alcoholism and an affair with his secretary swirled in the press during the 1900 strike, exacerbating the physical rigors of maintaining union solidarity in the widely scattered and volatile anthracite rank-and-file. But in a letter, Mitchell wrote, "I am going to stay with the boys until they succeed or fail; and if they fail I shall join

An illustration capturing the first trip by the Stourbridge Lion in 1829 — the first locomotive in America to run on a commercial railroad. When the locomotive was set into motion, it pushed the iron ribbon running surface a half inch into the wooden rails. .

the ancient order of has-beens and used-to-be's, and become one of its most revered members."

The union's new demands included a 20 percent increase in wages, the workday reduced from ten hours to eight, and fairer methods of measuring the coal they mined. Most importantly, it restated the call for recognition of the UMWA as the collective bargaining agent for the anthracite workers. Though this concession was frequently the silver bullet shot into the heart of a strike, without it John Mitchell knew the miners would always be vulnerable to working and living condition abuses.

The presidents of the coal and railroad companies rejected Mitchell's demands unequivocally. They countered that the union was unable to discipline its members, which made it irrelevant as a representative, and that it deprived non-union citizens of their right to seek mining work, which made it a criminal organization. The operators were equally unified in their resolve not to concede again to John Mitchell, and recommended the 1900 contract remain in force until 1903.

Thus the stage was set for what would be called the "most desperate fight capital and labor had ever engaged in." Upon that stage, a minstrel miner gleefully sang, "Just break the news to Morgan, that great official organ, tell 'em we want an increase in our pay. Just say we are united, and all our wrongs be righted, And with the company store we'll do away."

SHORT STORIES FROM THE MINES

The Pot And The Kettle

An important difference between anthracite and bituminous mining was that ultimately almost all anthracite deposits became owned by railroads. Before 1870, charters granted to anthracite railroads prohibited ownership of coalfields. Under pressure from the Philadelphia and Reading Railroad, however, the state of Pennsylvania changed its law, and permitted railroads to own coal lands. Legislators were aware they were giving monopolies to particular railroads, and to allow them to own and transport coal could create a tremendous economic power that might be used to gouge consumers and take advantage of miners.

However, George Baer believed that the UMWA was the monopoly. Baer said in his closing summation at the Anthracite Coal Strike Hearing, "The

facts are before us. The United Mine Workers have created a monster monopoly. They did shut up the anthracite mines for more than five months. They did conduct themselves in a lawless and criminal manner. They taxed the bituminous miners, and all laborers over whom organized labor has control, with a strike fund."

Mitchell's Ace In The Hole

Anti-union activists accused the Irishmen tried as Molly Maguires of employing a union to murder citizens and destroy private property. This perception evolved through the latter 19th century to represent unions as foreign organizations associated with perceived negative philosophies that should not exist in America, such as Socialism, Anarchism and Communism.

However, public opinion changed to support labor's right to organize. The UMWA's success in its 1900 strike coincided with tremendous growth of unions. Industrialists outside the anthracite industry respected John Mitchell because he never leveraged labor conflict as a class war. Mitchell promoted trade agreements to achieve equality between capital and labor, encouraging trade

agreements in industries such as railroads, publishing, shipping, iron molding, and construction.

Of course, Mitchell knew it was important to have the politicians on your side, and 1900 was a national election year. Labor strife could have jeopardized the Republican Party's efforts to re-elect President McKinley. Two years later, the coal operators ignored Mitchell's trade agreement evangelism, hastening the Great Strike of 1902.

Thugs And Goons, Inc.

The northeastern part of Pennsylvania in the post-Civil War era was among the most lawless, wild places in America. The anthracite mine owners formed the Coal and Iron Police because there was a vacuum in the local authorities. The owners viewed the force as a means to protect their coal and iron property. Once the Coal and Iron Police were formed, the companies could enforce their will over their workers by force. These were rough people for a rough time in a rough environment.

At the Lattimer Massacre, this security force simply fired on unarmed immigrants marching peacefully from one town to another trying to make an impression and get their side of the story told in public. And while many believe the fix was on before the doors of the courtroom even opened, the tragedy led to unifying the anthracite miners across ethnic lines, and would be the catalyst needed to galvanize unionization.

Attorneys for the coal and railroad companies called John Mitchell to testify before anthracite strike commission first in order to discredit him and thereby diminish the credibility of the strike and of the striking miners.

TAKE THE A TRAIN

As the anthracite industry matured, transporting hard coal became more profitable than mining it. Therefore, unlike in the bituminous fields, railroads began to buy up anthracite rights and buy out smaller mining concerns. By 1902, the railroads owned virtually all the anthracite deposits in northeastern Pennsylvania. In doing so they created the most technically advanced railroad system on earth.

At the beginning of the 19th century, England was the world's only reliable supplier of all-iron rails, and America's fledgling railroads were its biggest clients. These railroads had their earliest origins in northeastern Pennsylvania. The Stourbridge Lion was the first steam engine locomotive to run in America, and the Honesdale and Mauch Chunk gravity railroads were the first working freight systems, transporting anthracite from mines to waterway terminals.

By 1850, the Montour rolling mill in Danville and the Lackawanna Coal and Iron Company in Scranton were ending English dominance in iron rail manufacturing when they employed anthracite in iron smelting to mass-produce T-rails in this country in notable quantities for the first time. Before the century ended, America would possess 70% of all the railroads in the world.

By 1900, America generated more than 70% of its energy needs from coal, and only 2% from oil, giving the miner's union a very powerful influence throughout state and federal government.

THE COAL INDUSTRY IS AN ESSENTIAL PUBLIC SERVICE, AND YOUR
PROTRACTED LABOR DISPUTE HAS BECOME A NATIONAL MENACE THAT
IS STEERING THE COUNTRY ON COURSE WITH CALAMITY.
—President Theodore Roosevelt

CHAPTER 5

When nearly 150,000 anthracite members of the United Mine Workers of America went on strike on May 12, 1902, there was no such thing as a World Series or a World War. For five months, an absence of anthracite coal created a national industrial crisis affecting millions of people in the United States. The strike would become the longest and largest labor conflict in history, and revealed that America, the vanguard of modern progress, was in reality a bastion of industrial feudalism.

The strike held the country's attention from its beginning. Editorials appearing in newspapers across the country initially portrayed the United Mine Workers as a monopoly capable of regulating the availability of a strategic resource by controlling anthracite mining's labor supply. In letters to the editor, citizens volunteered their assistance to end the strike by, among other things, preaching Christ to the miners and watching the equipment while they were off the job.

The Lackawanna County Courthouse and the courthouse square in Scranton, Pennsylvania, at the time of the Anthracite Coal Strike Commission hearing in late 1902.

Smoke ordinances were violated and coal haze began appearing over cities because replacement bituminous coal burned dirtier than anthracite. Fashionable men at the beaches began wearing black derbies instead of Panama hats, which the airborne soot soiled. However, as pollution spread across America's cities, so did public concern.

By the end of the strike's first month, critical manufacturing processes were affected, like food preparation and iron smelting. Factories started shutting down because power producing steam boilers were fired by anthracite. Stores stopped receiving goods. Unemployment rose. Seven hundred people lost their jobs when the New Haven Iron and Steel Company closed. High coal prices docked steamboats servicing Long Island's oyster industry. Fruit growers suffered losses due to a lack of anthracite for evaporating purposes. Railroads stopped service because hard coal fueled steam locomotives. Hospitals and schools closed. Chicago's Fulton Market shut down when it could not get anthracite, and 200,000 people in the city lost their food supply. People there began stealing wooden street blocks for firewood. Baltimore enlisted men to go to northeastern Pennsylvania and mine anthracite for the city.

As fate would have it, in 1902 the Midwest and Northeast experienced their wettest and coldest June in years. By the end of the month, newspaper reports began focusing more on the dangerous conditions in the anthracite mines and the miserable living conditions in the company towns. Editorials now began criticizing operators for a blatant disregard for the public's welfare. One read: "The tactics of the petty nabobs of Lehigh are more like the antics of the old time Russian despots in dealing with their serfs, than the conduct of American employers towards American workingmen."

While the debate of sustaining capitalism at the expense of the working man raged in newspapers, tempers raged in the anthracite region as the coal operators tried to replace striking workers with non-union labor, called "scabs" by union members. Striking miners retaliated against the non-union laborers directly, or by dynamiting property like railroad bridges, breakers and offices. In the course of these violent reprisals, people were killed on both sides of the picket line. Pennsylvania's governor ordered the National Guard into the region to restore or maintain order.

An advertisement for milk indicates John Mitchell's popularity in the anthracite region.

As the 19th century gave way to the 20th, and spring turned to fall, the anthracite coal famine produced a national political hurricane. At its center was President Theodore Roosevelt. Roosevelt became president when William McKinley was assassinated in Buffalo, New York almost a year earlier, in September of 1901. Roosevelt was compelled to address the situation when Republican politicians came to him with concerns about the press's speculations that their party remained indifferent to the American public's plight.

The operators hoped that violence in the anthracite mines, and the strike's continental impact, would fuel public anger toward the striking miners, and compel Roosevelt to introduce the army into the region to protect collieries and replacement workers in the same way that President Grover Cleveland did in the Pullman strike in 1894 and President Rutherford Hayes did in railroad strikes in 1877. Though detailed reports from the Attorney General and the Commissioner of Labor and identified the grave inequities and historical injustices existing in the anthracite industry, they also stipulated that Roosevelt had no constitutional authority to end the strike.

Roosevelt did not want to conquer concentrated economic power, only to reform it through socially responsible federal regulation to achieve efficiency and invention without menacing

workers and consumers. A 1902 editorial in the Scranton Times laid the gauntlet at his doorstep: "The evils which the President must ask Congress to regulate are over-capitalization, discrimination in prices to destroy competition, insufficient personal responsibility of officers and directors, and the disregard of the rights of the people".

Believing he had to do something to avert a fuel shortage throughout the voter-rich eastern seaboard, Theodore Roosevelt invited John Mitchell and George Baer to meet with him in Washington on October 3rd, 1902 to discuss a resolution to the anthracite coal strike. This meeting was held while Roosevelt was recuperating in a private residence from a nearly fatal trolley accident because, in an ironic twist, union plasterers had not yet completed renovations to the White House. Never before had capital and labor met with an American president to resolve a labor dispute.

Roosevelt would write in his autobiography that he implored Baer and Mitchell to end the strike for the good of the country. He remarked, "I appeal to your patriotism and to the spirit that sinks personal consideration and makes individual sacrifices for the general good". Baer represented the interests of the coal and rail operators in an uncompromising manner, and likely was gathering first-hand information about the President's feelings for J.P. Morgan. Unlike Baer, though, John

1895
The Lehigh district boasts 63 UMWA locals, and sends ten delegates to the national convention.

1896
Nearly thirty years after the initial passage of mine safety laws in Pennsylvania, 502 workers still die in anthracite operations.

1896
The first motion picture is projected by a Vitagraph machine in a New York City theater.

1897
The Lattimer massacre occurs.

1898
Bituminous production in the U.S. is nearly nine times greater than anthracite mining.

Mitchell's calm demeanor impressed Roosevelt. "There was only one man in that conference that behaved like a gentleman," Roosevelt wrote of Mitchell, "and that man was not I." Ten days after the President found George Baer's loyalty to J.P. Morgan unflinching, he invited Morgan himself to Washington to personally discuss the strike.

On October 13th, 1902, with cold weather only weeks away, the American public waited as the President of the United States met with the architect of the anthracite trust. In their meeting, the President may have agreed to send troops into the anthracite collieries—but not to protect them. J.P. Morgan might have felt he had a better chance in a courtroom against the miners than on a battlefield against Theodore Roosevelt, because the following day the coal and railroad company presidents publicly agreed to the first federal arbitration of a labor dispute. John Mitchell ordered the nearly 150,000 striking miners to end their 164 day strike and return to the collieries. The strike cost the coal and railroad companies at least 70 million dollars in revenue, workers 25 million dollars in wages, and the UMWA nearly two million dollars in relief funds.

By the end of October, Roosevelt had impaneled the Anthracite Coal Strike Commission, and sent them to begin the hearing in Scranton. The Commission was composed of seven experts on various issues relating to the strike. It included the Secretary of Labor, a foreign diplomat, the retired head of the U.S. Army Corps of Engineers, a Bishop from Illinois, a mine owner, the editor of a mining industry journal, and the chief of the railway conductor's union. These men were charged with investigating the causes of the strike, and recommending a binding award based on

their findings. They began their investigation in northeastern Pennsylvania on October 30th, 1902 by touring company towns and descending into the anthracite mines.

John Mitchell assembled a team to prepare material for presentation before the commission. It included economists, publicists, investigators and secretaries. Although the hearing was a court proceeding, it would not follow the rules of evidence or other trial procedures. As the miner's lead counsel, Mitchell hired a young Clarence Darrow, despite Darrow's lack of knowledge of mining. Mitchell chose Darrow in part because of the outstanding reputation of his courtroom skills. He believed that Darrow's presence in this setting would overwhelm the opposition.

What worried Mitchell was Darrow's reputation in the minds of some politicians and newspaper editors as a radical socialist organizer. Darrow

(left) The governor of Pennsylvania ordered the National Guard into the anthracite region to deter violent reprisals by striking miners against coal and railroad personnel and property, and to also entice striking miners to break the picket line and return to work under the military's protection. (right)Photograph of the anthracite coal strike commission and attending lawyers for the striking miners and coal and railroad companies in courtroom number three of the Lackawanna County Courthouse. Clarence Darrow is marked as number 18, seen to the left of the center of the picture.

received national attention for participating in several previous labor conflicts, including defending Eugene Debs in the Pullman railway strike. Privately, Mitchell wondered if Darrow would employ his rising national prominence to encourage the growing presence of Socialism in American politics.

Two weeks after the Commission began their fact-finding tour in the anthracite region, the hearing began on November 14, 1902 in Courtroom Number Three in the Lackawanna County Courthouse. The courtroom was packed with newspaper reporters from all over the country, witnesses waiting to testify, and miners and mine owners from throughout the region. All six major railroad and coal companies were represented at the hearing, as well as 74 independent operators. There were so many people in the courtroom that some in the rear broke through a stain glass partition, and the hearing had to be stopped while the mess was cleaned and order restored.

Chief commissioner George Gray weakened the miner's united front on the first day when he ruled that non-union miners could be represented by their own counsel. Then the hearings began in dramatic fashion with a four and a half-day

During the 1902 strike, children would pick coal from slate piles and along railroad tracks to use at home for cooking and heating.

cross-examination of John Mitchell. Lawyers for the operators, including former U.S. Attorney General Wayne MacVeagh, attempted to intimidate and entrap Mitchell to diminish the miners' position. However, Mitchell's sharp wit and intelligent testimony left only respect in the minds of the commissioners, lawyers, and the press.

After calling well over 200 witnesses in five weeks, the commissioners asked Clarence Darrow to stop, and on December 22nd, 1902 they somberly convened the hearing for Christmas. The human rights abuses Darrow identified through the testimony he elicited from miners, miner's wives, and children, provided Americans across the country with their first awareness of the human rights violations occurring to these immigrants in anthracite region. However, the hearings would move to Philadelphia after a Christmas recess, and there the operators would have their turn to present their side of the conflict. John Mitchell and Clarence Darrow both knew that in the Pullman strike and the Homestead strike, the growing power of corporations defeated the unions. In the anthracite operators, the United Mine Workers were facing organized labor's most formidable opponent yet.

1898
J.P. Morgan and his associates reorganize their railroad holdings by interlocking directorates to control prices and increase profits.

1900
The United States returns to the gold standard.

1900
Women attain most legal rights, but still can't vote.

1900
Oldsmobile opens the first automobile factory in Detroit.

1900
Coal satisfies 71% of America's energy demands. Oil only accounts for 2%. 60% of anthracite coal is used for domestic cooking and heating.

INJUSTICE ANYWHERE IS A THREAT TO JUSTICE EVERYWHERE. WE ARE CAUGHT IN AN INESCAPABLE NETWORK OF MUTUALITY, TIED IN A SINGLE GARMENT OF DESTINY. WHATEVER AFFECTS ONE DIRECTLY, AFFECTS ALL INDIRECTLY. —Martin Luther King, Jr.

Letter from the Birmingham Jail, April 16, 1963

SHORT STORIES FROM THE MINES

The President Sets A Precendent
President Theodore Roosevelt described the Great Anthracite Coal Strike of 1902 as "a national menace to an essential public service that posed disastrous consequences for America". Despite having no legal justification to do so, he urged a commission be constituted to arbitrate a resolution to the strike. For the first time in its history, the American government intended to resolve a labor conflict in a way that protected the rights of both labor and capital.

John Mitchell publicly welcomed Roosevelt's arbitration offer. Summer was waning, and in September the strike entered its fourth month. While vacationing in Venice, Italy, J.P. Morgan publicly disclaimed any responsibility for the strike or its effects. The anthracite coal and railroad presidents patently rejected Roosevelt's arbitration offer. Instead, they instructed their mine superintendents to order miners back to

(below) America's industrial revolution may have been fueled by anthracite coal, but industrial advancement came late to the mining industry. Mules pulled loaded mine cars to the surface well into the 20th century. (right) Though the bituminous miners voted not to strike in solidarity with their anthracite counterparts, they did contribute a strike support fee of $1.00 per week. However, funds were not distributed quickly, and only the neediest miners were given assistance. Contributions to the UMWA strike fund were also received from children, and from as far away as England and Wales.

work by the second week in October. Any miner who did not return to work would be evicted from their company house, along with their family.

A Hard Life Gets Harder

Though it had made daily life across America more burdensome that it already was, nowhere was the 1902 strike's effect as formidable as in the already impoverished company towns. Reverend J. V. Hussie, Rector of St. Gabriel's Roman Catholic in the Scranton Diocese, remarked, "Conditions among the miners of the region are truly deplorable. The are barely able to exist. The homes cannot properly be called homes. They are habitations. The miners are frugal, conservative men, reasonable in their demands, and are a god fearing people. In sickness the miner is scarcely able to pay for medicine, and a death means a long-standing debt. Because of the poor wages received by the household head, it is impossible to keep the family together, and girls leave home as soon as they are able to work. Some of them go to other places to live as servants, and many of them go into the silk mills and other like industries. The boys go into the breaker as soon as they are able to toddle out of the house."

What I Really Meant To Say Was…

During the 1902 strike, George Baer received a letter from a Wilkes-Barre resident, William F. Clarke, suggesting that the frequency of strikes could be reduced if industrialists embraced Jesus Christ more into their affairs. Remarkably, Baer responded to the correspondence. Unfortunately for him, his letter eventually found its way into the national press and became known as the "Trustees of Providence" letter. In it, Baer wrote: "The rights and interests of the laboring man would be protected and cared for not by labor agitators, but by Christian men to whom God in his infinite wisdom has given control of the property interests of the country."

The American public may have accepted that the Rockefeller's, Astor's, and Vanderbilt's were its aristocracy, but it was not going to concede they were gods. Baer's letter evaporated any remaining public sympathy for the coal operators, and gave President Theodore Roosevelt the opportunity he needed to introduce the federal government into the donnybrook.

Theodore Roosevelt was the first U.S. president who envisioned the federal government as an umpire to protect the public interest in the conflicts involving capital, labor and the consumer.

UNPLANNED PRESIDENCY

Theodore Roosevelt's political conscience matured as the Progressive Era stimulated America's social consciousness. As New York's governor in 1899, he enacted taxes regulating industries directly affecting the public's welfare, like gas and transit corporations. "Speak softly and carry a big stick, and you will go far" was a West African proverb Roosevelt was fond of, and for him it would become a prophecy. The New York Republican Party so wanted T.R. out of the state's affairs it helped get him nominated as President McKinley's new vice-president in the 1900-reelection campaign. To their stupefaction, within a year McKinley would be dead and Roosevelt would be taking the presidential oath of office at the age of 42. He was now calling the stewards of the rail, oil and steel monopolies "malefactors of great wealth" and "consciousless swindlers" from the White House.

During the inaugural parade for Roosevelt's reelection in 1905, a band of coal miners carried a banner that read "We honor the man who settled our strike". In actuality, however, Roosevelt had an equally compelling political motivation for resolving the Great Anthracite Coal Strike of 1902. Republican congressional representatives from eastern seaboard states cautioned the President that the strike's effects were so widespread that the Party might lose numerous seats in Congress if it continued beyond the November mid-term election.

IT HAS COME TO THESE POOR MINERS TO BEAR THIS CROSS, YET
NOT FOR THEMSELVES. NOT THAT. BUT THAT THE HUMAN RACE MAY
BE LIFTED UP TO A HIGHER AND BROADER PLANE THAN IT HAS
EVER KNOWN BEFORE. —Clarence Darrow, lead counsel for the striking miners

CHAPTER 6

The Anthracite Coal Strike Commission reconvened in early January of 1903 to consider the operator's position. Over forty days it would witness a legal passion play produced by J.P. Morgan and directed by George Baer. Baer coordinated 28 lawyers for the coal and railroad corporations and independent operators to proclaim the unrestricted rights of capital and the individual worker, and the tyranny of organized labor. Reams of statistics were produced to accuse the United Mine Workers of conducting economic terrorism against America by restricting anthracite output. Corporate lawyers argued that a surplus of workers in hard coal country refuted Clarence Darrow's claim that wages and conditions were untenable.

In as rigorous detail as Clarence Darrow elicited from the miners and their families, George Baer

The Philadelphia & Reading Coal and Iron Company shipped more than nine million tons of anthracite coal by railroad in 1900, making it the largest mining operation in the region. The company was based in the town of Pottsville and operated almost exclusively in the Schuylkill region.

publicly branded the striking workers as a lineage of terrorists who employed violence and intimidation to prohibit free men from seeking work in the collieries. Baer said, "Today we have the spectacle of citizens born right in this country not being protected in their right to work, the very smallest of the national rights for the protection of which the government was founded. The whole power of our government must be brought to protect the man who wants to work and to strike down any and every hand that would oppress."

Everett Warren, counsel for the Pennsylvania Coal Company, also argued, "I do not dispute the right of men to organize, and I hold no brief against organized labor. The methods of the United Mine Workers, however, appear to be exquisitely adapted to degrade intelligent labor, to paralyze honest industry, to crush spirit, hope and ambition."

George Baer made capital's closing argument, of course. Clarence Darrow offered the summation for the miners. Baer spoke for two and a half hours from a written text. Darrow spoke for eight hours over two days, and did not refer to a single note. Despite his ideological conflicts with John

Mitchell about employing the miner's union to deliver the United States into a new era of social justice, Darrow ultimately confined his argument to the right of the immigrant miners and their families to what Darrow described as "the American standard of living."

When Darrow finished, John Mitchell stood up and walked over to the lawyers for the coal and railroad companies and shook their hands in a gesture designed to elicit one final sympathetic pose for the striking miners. Press reports detailing Mitchell's effective management of the miner's case before the Commission had elevated him to national celebrity. Political leaders in powerful Washington circles believed he was worthy of consideration as Theodore Roosevelt's running mate in the 1904 presidential election.

The Commissioners deliberated for a month after the adjournment. The hearing cost the federal government fifty-thousand dollars. More than ten thousand pages of transcripts were produced from the testimony of 558 witnesses during 74 days of proceedings. Most importantly, the hearing created a standard that the federal government

(left) The breakers no longer exist in northeastern Pennsylvania today, but the legacy of anthracite coal has made the region a case study of the immigrant experience in industrial sections of America. (right) Every miner's wife wondered if she would see her husband at the end of the day.

would employ in all future labor conflicts. It marks the first time that an American president intervened in a labor dispute in an even handed way, and therefore set a precedent that future presidents would ignore at their peril.

The Anthracite Coal Strike Commission released its report and award recommendations to the public on March 21st, 1903. Its nearly unanimous findings formed the first comprehensive study of the coal industry, and acknowledged that each side in the proceeding had merit to their arguments. The commission ruled that wages were inadequate to compensate for anthracite mining's dangerous working conditions, but the quality of life in anthracite communities was no worse

1900
Nearly every coal-producing state has passed mining regulations, but laws are uniformly unclear and not comprehensive.

1900
John Mitchell orchestrates a six-week strike that wins anthracite miners their first wage increase in more than two decades

1901
The New York Stock Exchange transacts 2 million trades for the first time. Four months afterward, it transacts 3 million trades.

1901
President McKinley is assassinated; Teddy Roosevelt succeeds McKinley.

1901
J.P. Morgan creates U.S. Steel, America's first billion dollar corporation.

YOU CAN KILL A MAN BUT YOU CAN'T
KILL AN IDEA. —Medgar Evers

WEATHER FORECAST.

Washington, March 21.—For Northeastern Pennsylvania, fair and not
so warm tonight; Sunday, fair.

4:00 EXTRA.

The Scranton Times.

Yesterday's Circulation:
21,300

34TH YEAR—NO. 69. **12 PAGES--SCRANTON, PA., SATURDAY AFTERNOON, MARCH 21, 1903.--12 PAGES** ONE CENT A COPY.

AWARD OF THE ANTHRACITE STRIKE COMMISSION.

TEN PER CENT. ADVANCE IN THE WAGES OF ALL MINE WORKERS

A Sliding Scale, One Per Cent. Raise for Every Five Cents on the Price of Coal Over $4.50, a Permanent Board of Conciliation.

THE COMMISSION'S AWARD IS TO LAST UNTIL MARCH 31, 1906

Washington, March 21.—The report of the anthracite strike commission was made public this morning. It provides in general for an increase of ten per cent. in the rate of wages paid contract miners and for a reduction in the hours per day of other mine workers. Water hoisting engineers are to work hereafter in eight-hour shifts, with a ten per cent. increase in wages where they have been working heretofore in such shifts. Other engineers and pumpmen are to have a five per cent. increase. Firemen are to have eight-hour shifts with-

the market conditions and kindred subjects. The hazardous nature of anthracite mining is dwelt upon, exhaustive statistics of accidents being presented. Sixty printed pages are devoted to the history and causes of the strike. This is followed by a detailed estimate of the losses accruing from the strike.

In the next chapter, covering the work of the commission, the report says: "All through their investigations and deliberations, the conviction has grown upon the commission that if they could evoke and con-

have eight-hour shifts, with the same pay which was effective in April, 1902; and where they are now working eight-hour shifts, the eight-hour shift shall be continued and these engineers shall have an increase of ten per cent. on the wages which were effective in April, 1902.

Hoisting engineers and pumpmen, other than those employed in hoisting water, who are employed in positions which are manned continuously, shall have an increase of ten per cent. on their earnings between November 1, 1902, and

hearing both parties to the controversy, and such evidence as may be laid before it by either party; and any award made by a majority of such board of conciliation shall be final and binding on all parties. If, however, the said board is unable to decide any question submitted, or point related thereto, that question or point shall be referred to an umpire to be appointed at the request of said board, by one of the circuit judges of the third judicial circuit of the United States, whose decision shall be final and binding in the premises.

The membership of said board shall at all times be kept complete, either the operators or miners' organizations having the right, at any time when a controversy is not pending, to change their representatives thereon.

At all hearings before said board the parties may be represented by such person or persons as they may respectively select.

No suspension of work shall take place, by lockout or strike, pending the adjudication of any matter so taken up for adjustment.

WAGES OF CHECK WEIGHMEN.

5.—The commission adjudges and awards: That whenever requested by a majority of the contract miners of any colliery, check weighmen, or check docking bosses, or both, shall be employed. The wages of said check weighmen and bosses shall be fixed, collected and paid by the miners in such manner as the said miners shall decide by a majority vote; and when requested by a majority of said miners, the operators shall pay the wages fixed for check weighmen and check docking bosses, out of deductions made proportionately from the earnings of the said miners on such basis as the majority of said miners shall determine.

DISTRIBUTION OF CARS.

6.—The commission adjudges and awards: That mine cars shall be distributed among miners, who are at work, as uniformly and as equitably as possible, and that there shall be no concerted effort on the part of the miners or mine workers of any colliery or collieries to limit the output of the mines, or to detract from the quality of the work performed, unless such limitation of output be in conformity with an agreement between an operator or operators and an organization representing a majority of said miners in his or their employ.

TOPPING OF CARS.

7.—The commission adjudges and awards: That in all cases where miners are paid by the car, where the increase

ployer or employe, shall not invalidate any of the provisions thereof.

GENERAL RECOMMENDATIONS.

Among the general recommendations with which the report concludes, the following are of particular weight and importance:

The practice of employing deputies upon request and at the expense of employers, instead of throwing the whole responsibility of preserving peace and protecting property upon the county and state officers, is one of doubtful wisdom, and perhaps, tends to invite conflicts between such officers and idle men, rather than avert them.

"The commission is constrained to decline making an award which would compel an agreement by the operators with the United Mine Workers of America; for, however importantly that order may have participated in the strike, it is not a party to this submission. Nor does the commission consider that the question of recognition of the United Mine Workers of America is within the scope of the jurisdiction conferred upon it by the submission. Whatever the jurisdiction of this commission, under the submission may be, the suggestion of a working agreement between employers and employes, embodying the doctrine of collective bargain, which is one the commission believes contains many hopeful elements —adjustment of the relations in the mining regions—but it does not see that, under the terms of the submission from which the powers of the commission are derived, such an agreement can be made to take the place of, or become part of its award.

"The commission agrees that a plan, under which all questions of difference between the employer and his employes shall first be considered in conference between the employer or his official representative and a committee chosen by his employes from their own ranks, is most likely to produce satisfactory results and harmonious relations."

ADJUSTMENT OF GRIEVANCES.

The commission has outlined a plan for the execution of trade agreements in the anthracite region, which is printed in the appendix. The report follows:

"The commission is of the opinion that some satisfactory method for the adjustment of grievances (the demand for which is embodied in the fourth claim) should be imposed by its award; and it supplies, therefore, the machinery for adjusting any disagreements that may arise under the award, along the lines demanded by the mine workers in a broader scope of applicability.

STANDARD OF LIVING.

The commission finds that the condi-

cruel as the boycott, and should be frowned down by all humane men."

GENERAL RECOMMENDATIONS.

COAL AND IRON POLICE.

"The employment of what are known as 'coal and iron policemen,' by the coal mining companies, while a necessity as things are, militates against the very purpose for which they are employed. Although the coal and iron policemen were men of good character, there were a sufficient number of bad characters to discredit the efforts of the whole body. Their presence is an irritant, and many of the disturbances in the coal regions during the strike grew out of their presence."

CHILD LABOR CONDEMNED.

The employment of immature children is condemned.

"In fact, they should be protected against the physical and moral influence of such employment, and there ought to be a more rigid enforcement of the laws which now exist."

AS TO COMPULSORY ARBITRATION.

The commission cannot see its way to recommend the adoption of compulsory arbitration.

"We do believe, however, that the state and federal governments should provide the machinery for what may be called the compulsory investigation of controversies when they arise."

The commission approves the plan of Charles Francis Adams, proposing an act to provide for the investigation of controversies affecting inter-state commerce, which authorizes the president to appoint a commission whenever the occasion may make such action necessary.

"With a few slight modifications, such an act would, in the opinion of the commission, meet justice and emergency as that which arose last summer in the anthracite coal regions, and we submit it to you for your consideration.

CONCLUSION.

than other industrial locations. The commission's major awards included a 10% wage increase for anthracite workers, the creation of a sliding scale to increase wages as prices increased, provisions to insure coal and mine cars were weighed fairly distributed equitably within a mine, and the rejection of a standardized ton because it was deemed impractical.

The commission found the issue of union recognition beyond its jurisdiction. Instead, it proposed a board of conciliation to review future grievances, composed of a judge and representatives for the miners and operators. The commission felt workers should have the right to join a union, and that collective bargaining was a suitable way to settle labor disputes. But it also supported "open shops" that provided non-union labor the opportunity to work.

Like the rest of the country following the hearing in the newspapers, the commission was aghast at the abuse of child labor in the anthracite mines and the enlistment of the Coal and Iron Police. Its recommendations formed the basis for the creation of the Pennsylvania State Police, the

(left) It would cost you a penny in March of 1903 to buy the Scranton Times to read about the Commission's arbitration decision. (right) With limited educational resources, most boys who lived in the anthracite coal fields understood that they would live their lives as a coal miner or laborer.

first state police organization in America, and helped refine the country's industrial policy by contributing to legislation protecting the right of a child to have a childhood. The country had grown.

The Great Anthracite Coal Strike of 1902 and the Anthracite Coal Strike Commission hearing also represented an important turning point in the history of organized labor in the United States. Before 1902, organized labor largely consisted of native born male skilled workers in various crafts. John Mitchell successfully integrated immigrant laborers into the labor movement. With Theodore Roosevelt lending his pressure on behalf of the United Mine Workers of America, the possibility for unionization in industrializing America became a reality.

Such industrial complexities existing in the United States as it entered the 20th century were never foreseen by the founding fathers. The Commission's findings demonstrated that the United States had matured into the world's preeminent superpower, and was ready to take on the challenges of the new century. America was unprepared to deal with monopolies, labor unions, child labor, and massive immigration. Hundreds of thousands of people came to northeastern Pennsylvania from 20 countries and were confronted with exploitation and danger. Not only did they survive, but they built dreams there that opened the golden door promised to them by the Statue of Liberty.

The Commission's report concluded with a warning that became a bearing for America as it journeyed into the 20th century: "Where production is controlled despotically by capital there may be a seeming prosperity, but the qualities which give sacredness and worth to life are enfeebled or destroyed. In the absence of a trustful and conciliatory disposition, the strife between capital and labor can not be composed by laws and contrivances. The causes from which it springs are as deep as man's nature, and nothing that is powerless to illumine the mind, and touch the heart, can reach the fountain head of the evil."

Though President William Howard Taft pursued twice as many antitrust suits in one term as Theodore Roosevelt did in two, Roosevelt's Anthracite Coal Strike Commission set a visionary precedent that redefined the relationship in America among organized labor, organized wealth and the federal government. And the stories from the mines it revealed will forever serve as a reminder that the most powerful advancements which we the people may achieve in the new millennium will still be inspired from the same respect for human dignity fought for a hundred years ago in the dangerous anthracite coal fields of northeastern Pennsylvania.

England enacted child labor legislation by 1796. It would be another hundred years before America began addressing the problem of child labor in anthracite mining.

STORIES FROM THE MINES

Who Would've Thought...

John Mitchell did not want to strike in 1902, and the presidents of the coal and railroad companies knew this. Mitchell even reduced some of the union's original demands early in the strike to facilitate a resolution. The industrialists viewed this as Mitchell's weakness, and believed the strike could be broken by encouraging the miners to defy their president and actually go on strike, which would force Mitchell to resign and leave the strikers without a leader. These industrialists also knew the UMWA did not have much of a strike fund, and, because the demand for coal was seasonal, believed the union would collapse before their coal and railroad companies had to ship anthracite to customers for the late fall and early winter of 1902.

The strike ended up lasting more than five months. What the coal and railroad company presidents didn't count on was John Mitchell abiding by the union's vote to strike, or a swing in public sympathy to the miners when the press began reporting the strike was called by the rank-and-file, and not by agitating union officials. In fact, 35,000 men from West Virginia, Alabama and Michigan joined the work stoppage. Ironically, though, UMWA members in the Lackawanna district, virtually ground zero for the anthracite industry, voted against the strike by a margin of 57% to 43%.

Anthracite Ballads

Wilkes-Barre native Con Carbon was a minstrel who performed anthracite ballads throughout the hard coal region. During the strike and the hearing, John Mitchell would invite him to perform at the strike's headquarters at the Hotel Hart in Wilkes-Barre. Two popular songs at the time were "A White Slave Of The Mine" and "The Miner's Fate."

A White Slave of the Mine

I am a little collier lad,
Hardworking all the day
From early morn till late at night
No time have I to play
Down in the bowels of the earth
Where no bright sun rays shine
You find me busy at my work
A white slave of the mine.

The Miner's' Fate

At just three o'clock in the morning
As the whistles gave the death sound
One hundred brave men that were mining
Were buried alive in the ground.
O, what can we do now to save them?
To rescue their bodies at least
O, help us, Great Father, we pray thee,
One poor soul to rescue at least.

COAL STRIKE

The Great Anthracite Coal Strike of 1902 drew the attention of the world. The Times Of London published this article after Roosevelt's failed meeting with George Baer and John Mitchell: "Every indication goes to support the belief that President Roosevelt has not abandoned his efforts to end the coal miners' strike and to relieve the country, so far as it is now possible, from the disaster which threatens it. It is reported this afternoon that the President has written or is about to write a letter to Mr. Mitchell, the president of the Miner's Union, appealing to him to end the strike by advising the miners to return to work on the understanding that Mr. Roosevelt will ask Congress to pass a National Arbitration Law. The Plan may succeed, but there are many things against it, including the circumstance that Mr. Mitchell's power over the strikers is now problematical. It is understood that he himself fears that he is about to lose control of them, and that more serious disorders than those which have

yet occurred in the mine region are imminent.

The effects of the strike will not only be felt in this country, but the British consumer also will suffer through having to pay higher prices. Orders for British coal are increasing every day, and the sale of 100,000 tons for America at Newscastle this afternoon will almost certainly be followed by even larger sales. As for the situation here, the trite expression need, I suppose, by the correspondent of every London paper here—'its seriousness cannot be overestimated'— is literally true."

(left) When John Mitchell died in September of 1919, he received only a sliver of an obituary in the New York Times, but in Scranton, where he requested he be laid to rest, the people waiting outside St. Peter's Cathedral to pay their last respects could not fit in the church. (right) The presidential appointed members of the Anthracite Coal Strike Commission moved from Scranton to Philadelphia to continue the hearing beginning in January, 1903

1901

By this time it is estimated that one billion tons of anthracite coal had been mined from northeastern Pennsylvania since 1820.

1902

Anthracite miners conduct the Great Anthracite Coal Strike of 1902. Nearly 150,000 mine workers stop work for more than five months to secure higher wages and fairer practices.

1902

Coal miners in France and Belgium strike for an eight hour work day.

1903

Boston beats Pittsburgh in first baseball World Series.

1903

The Wright Brothers conduct the first powered flight.

THE UNIVERSITY OF SCRANTON

There were never many options to working in the anthracite mines, and many, many boys followed their fathers into the pit, inheriting the likelihood of permanent physical disability and the daily possibility of being killed on the job. From its inception in 1868, the Diocese of Scranton sought to create a school that could provide young people with the chance to enter the region's business and professional community. By 1892, it had succeeded in opening St. Thomas College, thereby introducing a mostly immigrant population to the possibilities of higher education.

A core arts and humanities curriculum evolved under the administration of the Diocese first, the Xaverian Brothers for a few years and the Christian Brothers for more than 40 years. The first graduating class would produce five lawyers, six physicians and twelve priests or members of religious orders. A night school was also offered, which young breaker boys attended.

A local newspaper described northeastern Pennsylvania's earliest post-secondary school as "a college in which manhood is taught, in which boys are made manly, manly in body, manly in intellect, and manly in dealing with the world." A visiting academic remarked, "I like to come to Scranton. Though you have not erected monumental buildings, you have created monumental men."

In 1942, the Jesuits assumed administration of the school, and St. Thomas College became the University of Scranton, the 24th Jesuit College in the country. The University subsequently created an Institute of Industrial Relations that provided adult education program for regional union leaders. Today, the University of Scranton, conceived as a "university for the sons of workingmen" remains a leading co-educational, economic and cultural resource in northeasternPennsylvania.

The University of Scranton received a substantial image and resource upgrade when Mr. Worthington Scranton, grandson of one of Scranton's founders, donated in trust to the Diocese his family's estate and additional acreage in close proximity to the site of school. This included the homestead's Victorian mansion (below), which was initially used to house the Jesuits who taught at the school and has changed very little from its original construction in 1871.